"You are holding a gem! This richly inte[g] theology, business acumen, and spiritu[al] tians understand and live out their fait[h] [in the] workplace. Busenitz draws from a deep reservoir of entrepreneurial experience, a career as a business strategy scholar, and a vibrant Christian commitment to remind us that God is already present in our workplaces. When we begin with this recognition, our souls are shaped for God's purposes, allowing us to participate with God in bringing innovation, compassion, justice, and love to the workplace."

**—Denise Daniels, Hudson T. Harrison
Endowed Chair of Entrepreneurship
Business & Economics Department, Wheaton College**

"For years, I struggled with living out my faith in my work, trying to find clever ways to bring Christianity into my field and daily conversations. What I often didn't realize is that God was already there. Lowell Busenitz has written a tremendously helpful book for the entrepreneurially minded that invites readers into a 'with God' relationship in all things—including the sacred pursuit of their daily work."

—Jeff Haanen, Founder, Denver Institute for Faith & Work

"Lowell Busenitz has authored one of the most practical books I've encountered in the space of faith-based entrepreneurship. Leveraging a solid biblical framework, Lowell shows *how* we engage our faith in entrepreneurial pursuits and *how* God develops us spiritually through the experience. The soul work documented here explains why a creative God blesses us with innovation, where our spiritual gifts come to life in entrepreneurial work, how we love our neighbors through the work week, and when work becomes a platform for advancing compassionate justice. In addition, this book reframes the inevitable challenges, setbacks, and losses of work life in the context of spiritual maturity so that the 'valley of death' becomes a blessing a disguise. I encourage every Christian entrepreneur to read this book—not just for instruction in faith at work, but also for the inspiration that work makes us better Christ-followers."

—Chuck Proudfit, President, At Work on Purpose

"*Soul Work* is a breath of fresh air! So many invigorating insights about God in the workplace that I've never heard before. His book changed my theology of work."

—Michael Klassen, President, Illumify Media Global

"*Soul Work* is a beautiful reminder that while God calls us to create and do work for him, ultimately, our work is a means to a much bigger end—experiencing God and being with him."

—Jordan Raynor, national bestselling author of ***Called to Create*** **and** ***Master of One***

"Written by a scholar of entrepreneurism and innovation, *Soul Work* is a welcome gift to a maturing faith and work movement. *Soul Work* is theologically robust yet embodies on every page an accessible and refreshing down-to-earth practicality. The myriad of timeless insights along with reflective questions make this book a rich interactive experience for the reader who longs to better connect their Sunday faith with the joys and challenges of their Monday workplace. Anyone with an entrepreneurial interest or mindset will find a treasure trove of wisdom mined from years of experience and reflection by an author who brings his best game to this book. I highly recommend it."

—Tom Nelson, President, Made to Flourish
Author of ***Work Matters*** **and**
The Economics of Neighborly Love

"*Soul Work* is a timely book that focuses on the growing movement and resurgent interest in the intersection of faith and work. In this book, Dr. Lowell Busenitz addresses the most important issues of how and why to integrate faith and work. He also provides new insights into this topic through his God-Already-at-Work model, where he highlights issues of co-creation, giftedness, and encountering challenges. *Soul Work* provides relevant Scriptures, thought-provoking questions, and a comprehensive model. This book is a must for anyone who is anywhere along the entrepreneurial journey!"

—Brett Smith, Cintas Chair of Entrepreneurship
and Founding Director, Leading the Integration of
Faith & Entrepreneurship (L.I.F.E.)
Research Lab, Miami University, Ohio

"Many struggle to see anything spiritual in work. The latter is little more than what we do to get by, to earn a living, and to survive, but hardly a reality that awakens us to God and his purpose in our lives. In his excellent book, *Soul Work*, Lowell Busenitz responds to this distorted viewpoint and unpacks for us the profoundly spiritual and Christ-exalting nature of our work, and how it serves to connect us with God. If 'work' has become for you a purely mundane necessity, entirely detached from your personal relationship with the Lord, read this book to be set straight and put on the right track."

—Sam Storms, Lead Pastor of Preaching & Vision
Bridgeway Church, Oklahoma City

SOUL
WORK

SOUL WORK

FINDING GOD IN YOUR ENTREPRENEURIAL PURSUITS

LOWELL W. BUSENITZ

HENDRICKSON
PUBLISHERS

an imprint of Hendrickson Publishing Group

THEOLOGY OF WORK · PROJECT

Soul Work: Finding God in Your Entrepreneurial Pursuits

© 2023 Lowell Busenitz

Published by Hendrickson Publishers
an imprint of Hendrickson Publishing Group
Hendrickson Publishers, LLC
P. O. Box 3473
Peabody, Massachusetts 01961-3473
www.hendricksonpublishinggroup.com

ISBN 978-1-4964-7623-4

All rights reserved. No part of this book may be reproduced or transmitted in any form or by any means, electronic or mechanical, including photocopying, recording, or by any information storage and retrieval system, without permission in writing from the publisher.

Neither the publisher nor the author is responsible for, nor do they have any control over, the content of any third-party websites referenced in this book, whether at the time of the book's publication or in the future.

All Scripture quotations, unless otherwise indicated, are taken from the Holy Bible, New International Version®, NIV®. Copyright © 1973, 1978, 1984, 2011 by Biblica, Inc.™ Used by permission of Zondervan. All rights reserved worldwide. www.zondervan.com. The "NIV" and "New International Version" are trademarks registered in the United States Patent and Trademark Office by Biblica, Inc.™

Scripture quotations marked MSG are taken from THE MESSAGE, copyright © 1993, 2002, 2018 by Eugene H. Peterson. Used by permission of NavPress. All rights reserved. Represented by Tyndale House Publishers, Inc.

Scripture quotations marked (NLT) are taken from the Holy Bible, New Living Translation, copyright ©1996, 2004, 2015 by Tyndale House Foundation. Used by permission of Tyndale House Publishers, Carol Stream, Illinois 60188. All rights reserved.

Printed in the United States of America

First Printing — February 2023

This book is dedicated to my parents,
John and Frieda Busenitz, in great appreciation
for pointing me toward the One who saves my
soul and for teaching me the value of work.

I also dedicate this to you, the entrepreneurial
worker who longs for more of God.
I pray these writings will help you forge a more
soul-enhancing pathway forward.
A journey that moves you closer to God
is the only journey worth pursuing.

God's blessing on you and your work.

CONTENTS

INTRODUCTION

"As a part of a group of six business leaders, we meet once a month for a four-hour block to push one another and to hold one another accountable," said Lou, an entrepreneur and business owner. "We are owners and CEOs of entrepreneurial businesses, and we all hold similar spiritual values. We ask one another the tough questions like family priorities, whether to pursue a business expansion, handling tough employee challenges, moral issues, and spiritual values. Going on three years, we have become a tight-knit group."

At a recent meeting, one of the entrepreneurs in the group asked, "What if we pool some of our resources and do something to address a social problem like human trafficking or the homeless? I would like to see us do something that *really matters*."

I admire Lou's fellow business owner for wanting to give from his success. But the comment unknowingly separated the gospel into distinct work and charity spheres. Fighting social inequality employs the radical hospitality of the gospel, and so does everyday labor. Jesus' work as a teacher was important, and so was his carpentry work. It was not his financial contributions to the needy that saved souls—it was his fellowship with them.

Our work, then, can become a place to discover and connect directly with God. Instead of taking God to work, God is already there and embedded in our work. His presence awaits you there. With the eye-opening guidance of the Holy Spirit, work can become a rich place to know and experience God more intimately.

Consider a question from my friend Jake. "Am I wasting time building my career with little explicit eternal value? I have a full plate with my work, and I rarely see how it connects with my spiritual interest." Unfortunately, this is frequently how believers view work. If, like Jake, you're pursuing a relationship with God, then you're probably battling with how your work fits with your spiritual journey. You may even feel like work is a spiritual opponent.

Work was first God's idea. After creating the heavens and the earth, Genesis 2:2 says, "And on the seventh day God finished his work." Then God put Adam and Eve in the Garden of Eden and told them to "work it and take care of it" (Gen. 2:15). Because we are made in God's image, this means we are designed to work. Working is a part of our DNA. Unfortunately, it's often seen as disruptive to our spiritual journey. This book is about a different way where work is embraced as a place to discover a rich and engaging God.

My Story

I was born into a family of six boys and one girl in rural Kansas, where my parents were grain and livestock farmers. By kindergarten age, I was bringing wood into the house for tomorrow's heat and helping in the garden with pulling weeds and harvesting potatoes before playtime.

My days started with my father calling up the stairs at 6:00 a.m., "Boys, time to get up." If I was slow in waking up, my oldest brother would soon call to me "Lowell, your cow is calling" until I responded. Work was central to the enterprise, and we all had our part to do.

My parents' faith was very important to them. As active participants in a Mennonite faith community, we regularly prayed for the needs of the day. Sunday was set aside as a day of rest, and we usually attended two church services. Our faith community shared a strong missional orientation, and from the fruits of our labor, full-time ministries were supported.

My early years of work provided many experiences, skill development opportunities, questions, challenges, and yes, even glimpses of God. I recall getting on a horse to ride the cattle in from the wheat pasture on brisk December mornings while enjoying the open horizon and sunrises. I remember planting seeds in my own prepared garden, watching new sprouts poke up through the soil crust. I learned about soil erosion and caring for the land, watched fresh rain revitalize drought-stricken crops, and the art and science of caring for our livestock. When called on to shovel "itchy" grain or work in cold and windy conditions, I would often connect work to Adam and Eve's sin and think about the resulting curse.

In my formative college years, I experienced meaningful relationships and engaged with leadership. By my last two years of college, I had finally learned how to become decent student. It was during these years when the longing for a deeper relationship with God really emerged. After graduation, I joined InterVarsity Christian Fellowship in campus ministry working with student leaders, conducting training workshops, and organizing conferences.

After six years with InterVarsity, I began working in the construction industry. After one year, I started my own business and learned about taking care of customers, dealing with competition, bidding on new projects, and developing my own skill set. Entrepreneurship stretched me in multiple ways.

As I found that the construction industry was not going to hold my attention for the rest of my working years, I decided to pursue graduate studies in strategic management and entrepreneurship. This journey pushed me substantially beyond anything I could have ever imagined.

Upon completion of my PhD from Texas A&M University, I became a professor of strategic management at the University of Houston. After six years, I moved to the University of Oklahoma where I cofounded the entrepreneurship program in the Price College of Business. My research continued to gain traction, and I had the great privilege of walking alongside hundreds of learners in entrepreneurship and their development of business concepts.

In the years following my student ministry days, I often wrestled with the worth of my work spiritually. But in God's grace, he sometimes brought me enough understanding to see his "imprints" in the work of my hands and mind. These "God-touches" left me pondering spirituality in fresh ways. Eventually, the workplace became a place of opportunity to discover and connect with God—in fact, I discovered that God was already present in my workplace.

As a teenager, I had already started reasoning that if faith is real, then it should be equally relevant across all of life, not just church life. My relationship with God should be just as relevant in my work life as in leading a Bible study or doing "ministry." By God's grace, I discovered him to be abundantly present in the workplace. Furthermore, this revelation enabled me to thrive by discovering the interconnectedness and complementariness of my work and my spiritual life.

Is This Book for You?

At a recent conference on faith and work, Stuart shared some of the positive influences he was able to have as an entrepreneur and a city council member. Then Pastor Tracy, the leader of the panel, asked him, "How is your work impacting your relationship with God?" After a significant pause, Stuart said, "I'm going to need to get back with you on this."

Like Stuart, most of us have given little or no thought to such a question. Along my pathway, I came to realize that God is the creator and sustainer of our world and lives and that he is already everywhere present. The touches of our hands and minds are potential connections for us to God. He wants us to link in with him.

Are you desirous of some serious soul work but there seems to be a chasm between your work and spiritual life? Maybe you're struggling to make sense of your work at a spiritual level. Maybe you're on a journey toward God, but a personal relationship with him still seems elusive. If you desire to understand God better, then work can be a channel for discovering him. The everywhere-present God is more than ready to connect with you! Given that you picked up this book, you most likely have a desire for some soul growth, or you're not satisfied with the proximity of your spiritual journey. Welcome!

In full disclosure, my pathway to God is through Jesus Christ. He is alive within me, and he is my lover, my advocate, my guide, my brother, my strength, my redeemer in ever-increasing ways. My relationship with God through Jesus is at the core of my life. He is my eternal hope. But I am still young in my journey and have so much to learn.

If you've been embarking on a different pathway to God, I still invite you into this book. This doesn't change the fact that God is present in our places of work. We all have much to learn with coming to know God. Regardless of your current position and leanings, I invite you to join us into this journey of soul work. You'll find God waiting to connect with you at your work.

This book offers a new way of thinking about your work, a new paradigm for how you can meet God at work. Work is like a rich resource pool of opportunities for letting God come and touch you. By the power of the Holy Spirit, discovering God in your workplace is possible beyond anything you have ever imagined! I pray you can increasingly connect with the God who longs to connect with you.

What's Ahead in this Book?

Part I of this book (chapters 1–3), "Discovering God Already at Work," establishes the biblical premise for the new paradigm from which I'm building. Chapter 1 notes the most common ways work is viewed by Christians today. I characterize this as the "faith-to-work" model where we take spiritual values into the workplace. These often include practices like prayer, good ethics, meditations, the Holy Spirit's counsel in decision making, and loving one another, among others. However, such practices, while good, often struggle to encourage much spiritual growth. This chapter will identify the spiritual voids most of us feel in our workplaces.

Chapter 2 presents the "God-Already-at-Work" model as the new paradigm from which the entire book builds. Work is a great context for pointing us to God and constructively enabling soul work in connecting us to God. This chapter provides the foundation for understanding this practical approach for discovering God already in your work.

Drawing on both the Old and New Testaments, chapter 3 lays the biblical foundation for our work. It moves us beyond a common understanding of work because of the fall. The Scriptures point us to consider God's creation and his presence in our work, in how he values our work, and how he connects with us through our work.

Part II of the book (chapters 4–8), "Opportunities for Experiencing God at Work," establishes five spiritual work disciplines for finding God in our entrepreneurial and business endeavors. Chapter 4 delves into the innovation and co-creating processes common to entrepreneurial pursuits. Because we are made in God's image, we have the privilege of innovating and extending what God has created to develop for the good of life on this earth. Furthermore, for those who have eyes to see, engaging in innovation can enable us to discover the deeper thumbprints of God in what he created.

Chapter 5 unwraps the relevance of our spiritual giftedness for our work. Far too often, our spiritual gifts are limited to the church context. Just as our spiritual life doesn't need to stop when we enter the workplace, neither does our giftedness. Becoming a light of our God in the workplace usually finds its roots in our individual giftedness. Engaging our work from a position of our giftedness opens our eyes to see God and pursue promising opportunities.

Chapter 6 focuses on seeing God in and through our "neighbors." The gain of this chapter is in seeing God in the many and varied individuals with whom we engage. The practice of loving our neighbors at work becomes a channel for seeing God's imprint in creating all humankind in his image. In so doing, we deepen our solidarity with God. We also get to see the good that God has put in each of us as we pursue goodness for others.

Chapter 7 addresses the pursuit of justice. Injustices in the workplace are commonplace. However, with injustices also come opportunities to address the wrongs and the hurting to help contribute to the common good. Doing so can connect us to the God of justice who cares far more than we do. God's purity and ultimate justice gives us an anchoring hope. The benefit of this chapter is in its offering of constructive channels for helping with the practice of justice and in so doing unite with the heart of God more closely.

Chapter 8 probes the pain issues we encounter in our businesses. Dealing with challenges such as lying, competitors, failed dreams, false accusations, stolen ideas, flaws in our legal system, and coworker conflicts are painful realities. When going through our "Valley of Death," we invariably have the opportunity to engage in some serious soul work.

In Part III, "The Fruit of Being with God at Work," which includes chapters 9 and 10, we will discuss how worship is the climax of uniting with God in and through our work. In the context of chapters 4–8, we now consider the implications of recognizing the nature and character of our God more explicitly. When we see glimpses of God already at work, we want to respond in worship. The Hebrew word *avodah* or the root of it appears many times in the Old Testament. Sometimes it means "work" or "service," sometimes it means "worship," and sometimes it means both. *Avodah* is "work" and "worship" overlapping in meaning and sometimes becoming indistinguishable!

Chapter 10 puts the capstone on work as a central opportunity for spiritual formation. Spiritual disciplines are like resources facilitating the building of our souls to connect us with our God who is already at work. They are pathways to the real presence of God among us. While our workplaces are notoriously challenging, we can prepare the way for some serious soul work within. Our work can become a thriving space for knowing God.

As you progress through this book, each chapter starts with a prayer. I will continue to bring these prayers before the Lord on your behalf. Maybe you would also like to take a few moments before reading each chapter to make these prayers your own. The Spirit of the Lord be with you!

PART I

DISCOVERING GOD ALREADY AT WORK

1

STRIVING TO CONNECT GOD AND WORK

Gracious and loving Heavenly Father, in love you spoke me into being before the foundation of the world. Your love has surrounded me and patiently nudged me forward into greater intimacy with you. Thank you for how you have used work to deepen my journey with you. Holy Spirit, come now and guide these words to fill our minds with you so we can know you more intimately. Amen.

The Great Divide

"Why are those who seem most interested in spiritual issues the ones who often go on to full-time ministry?" This is a question I asked of my teacher one Sunday morning when I was seventeen. "It seems those with more spiritual interests are less likely to pursue vocational alternatives," I continued. Behind my inquiry was a wrestling with the reality of God's presence. I thought to myself, "If I really want to grow in knowing God, will I be disadvantaged by pursuing a vocational direction not in full-time ministry?"

I had already tasted the Lord's presence, but it was becoming apparent that I was only at the tip of the iceberg. I longed for more. Did my career track matter in this regard? Should my level of spiritual interest drive my career path? Although my budding biblical perspective was pointing me toward a God who was equally relevant across all vocations, was what I thought really true?

From early in my life, I learned work could be good. Of course, it was also necessary for making a living. From the proceeds of work, we are able to eat, go to school, support family, and serve others. It was largely unspoken, but self-respect and good things also come from work.

My earliest encounter with entrepreneurial work came when I was eight years old in 1960. Taking clues from my mom's large garden, I carved out my own plot of land. After a spring and summer of tilling the soil and caring for my plants, the highlight of the year came when I loaded up my harvested pumpkins to offer them to a local grocer. I still vividly remember my exchange with the store manager and the moment he handed me a check for $2.60 (which today is about $10!) in exchange for the seven pumpkins. My first entrepreneurial endeavor had earned a nice return.

I felt a sense of accomplishment and dignity from this gardening effort, and I realized that work could indeed be good. But was there any spiritual significance to it? Except for when it rained on parched soil, I rarely gave more than a passing thought to how my everyday work could be relevant for my journey in growing toward God.

God graciously guided me through my challenges and misperceptions. By his grace, I've seen the reality of his presence meaningfully penetrating my work. I now see God as present in *all my life*. Furthermore, work has become an incredibly valuable channel for coming into a closer union with him.

Do you struggle with finding God in your work? Are you frustrated when work seems to get in the way of your relationship with God? Consider an alternative of journeying with me in this book as it charts a course for us both through opportunity to engage with the living God through your work.

The "God touches" I've experienced in my work resulted in significant steps forward, and I now realize that he has been more powerfully present in my work than I once could have ever imagined. If we believe that God is already present in our workplaces, then we will realize how our work can become transformative and draw us into a more beautiful intimacy with him.

Vocations in the Scriptures

As God reveals himself to me (and to all of humankind), I'm particularly impacted by my reflections of the workplace in the Scriptures. To illustrate God's clear interest in our vocations, let's consider the following vocations mentioned in the Scriptures with modern-day counterparts:

- *Carpenters and woodworkers:* God gave Bezalel the Spirit of God and the skill in woodwork and craftsmanship to build the furnishings of the Tabernacle (Exod 31:2–4), and many were involved in building David's house (2 Sam. 5:11). Jesus learned the construction trade from Joseph (Matt. 13:55; Mark 6:3).

- *International businesspeople:* Solomon was a business entrepreneur involved in international trade and merchant ships (1 Kings 10:22–29; 2 Chron. 9:13–14). He also had profitable partnerships with kings and queens (1 Kings 10:1–13). Ultimately, though, his great wisdom and the resulting work and wealth gave way to arrogance and diversion and away from his union with God.

- *Merchants:* There were entrepreneurs in the marketplace; some did well and were spoken of appreciatively (2 Chron. 9:13–14; Song 3:6), while others were called out for dishonest gain (Hos. 12:7; Rev. 12:15). Lydia, the "dealer in purple cloth" from Thyatira, was likely an accomplished and influential entrepreneur. She was also Paul's first convert in Philippi (Acts 16:14–15, 40).

- *Doctors and nurses:* There were physicians who embalmed Joseph's father, Jacob (Gen. 50:2). There were midwives in the birthing of babies (Exod. 1:15–21). Nurses were often honored positions (2 Sam. 4:4; 2 Kings 11:2; Gen. 24:59; 35:8). There were doctors who tried to cure people (Mark 5:25–26). Luke, the writer of his Gospel and Acts, was a physician (Col 4:14).

- *Teachers:* There were those who taught the next generations (Exod. 18:20; Col. 3:16), and teaching was also identified as a spiritual gift (1 Cor. 12:28; Rom. 12:6–7).

- *Night watchmen/security personnel:* There were guards and those who protected the cities from violence (2 Sam. 18:24–27; Isa. 21:11–12; Ps. 127:1).

- *Urban (re)developers:* Nehemiah was very entrepreneurial in the gathering of resources and managing the rebuilding of the wall (see the book of Nehemiah).

- *Administrators and government leaders:* Although enslaved under enemy nations, Joseph, Mordecai, and Daniel used their appointments as government leaders to serve the Lord and the people of Israel, which led to pivotal turns in history (Gen. 41:37ff.; Est. 6–10; Dan. 5; the "city clerk" in Acts 19:35). Joseph was deeply touched by his work and later recognized God's great "good."

From these examples, it's apparent that God's purposes for us don't hinge on whether we're in full-time ministry. In God's economy, one career is not more sacred than another. The relevance and vitality of knowing God and the potential of his presence is available in all careers. What is rarely addressed is how work can become a channel for enabling spiritual flourishing.

Linking God and Work

In my early adult years, I understood human flourishing to come through praying, meditating on the Scriptures, collective worship, loving one another, communicating the message of God to others in my workplace, practicing strong ethics, and so on. To this day, my soul continues to find nourishment as I engage in these practices.

Then, when I was in my early thirties, some subtle shifts started taking place in my life. As an entrepreneur in the construction industry, I became intrigued with the different kinds of wood and the importance of the right wood for various applications. For example, I discovered that while yellow pine is strong for structural purposes, it also quickly rots if subjected to moisture, but cedar and redwood can handle years of exposure to the outdoor elements. For interior applications, I found out that the variations between open and closed grain woods impact the way they absorb stain and that the style of the grain also helps to set the desired tone for a room. The density and hardness of different woods also have implications for milling and use.

Contemplating God's creation of all these different trees from which we get our wood can be amazing. And the more I worked with specific wood, the more the various properties and nuances became evident. However, my fascination with different types of wood hardly touched my spiritual journey. Little did I realize that what I was working with all day long could be a means of connecting me to God, yet my growing amazement with different wood became a foretaste of more to come as I began to wonder if the work of my hands could become a way of opening some windows to God and thereby enriching my spiritual journey.

Clearly, practicing the spiritual disciplines of my morning quiet times, prayer, collective worship, and service to others continue to be instrumental in my growth. But the breeze of the Holy Spirit was now starting to blow into my work life. At some point, I started noticing that the most impactful advancements in my relationship with the Lord came through my work as an entrepreneur and then as an entrepreneurship professor.

I've also had the privilege of watching numerous entrepreneurs make significant spiritual strides forward in the context of high work demands. It's always a delight to see their giftedness come alive in their innovative thinking, building organizations, utilizing their unique skill sets, becoming teachers, and so forth.

I now see that work can be an amazing context for advancing our spiritual journeys—though unfortunately, most of these

opportunities tend to be overlooked. This book therefore seeks to
help you open your own window to knowing God more intimately
in and through your work. Since God is everywhere present, this
means that he is *present everywhere*—much more present than most
of us realize.

Challenges with Faith at Work

Let's now talk about some realities. There have long been significant challenges to meeting God in the workplace. When our
spiritual life is seen as separate from our daily work, this is commonly characterized as the sacred/secular divide or dualism.[1] Until
we're individually able to dissolve this dichotomy, our spiritual advancement through work will be seriously impeded.

For centuries, Christians tended to think of their daily work only
as something they did just to put food on the table—the only ones
who "worked for God" were the clergy. Then along came the Refor-
mation in sixteenth-century Germany and Reformers such as Martin Luther (1483–1546)[2] and John Calvin (1509–1564) gave spiritual
worth to even the smallest of duties. Calvin reminded us that just as
the Spirit of God was the one who gave Bezalel the ability to craft the
furnishings of the Tabernacle, God is the one who gives us the ability
and skills to perform our work.[3] Luther and Calvin both taught that
we have vocational callings to serve God and to be "the salt in the
earth" (Matt. 5:13), and their teaching served to open the door for us
to see the dignity and spiritual significance of ordinary work.

Regardless, some people still feel that pursuing a ministry career is of the highest significance. After all, what could possibly be
more important than explicitly being involved with people's spiritual lives? For those not in full-time ministry, they feel that their
work is just what they do to make a living, but they can justify doing
what they do if they can contribute financial or material support
to those with a "higher calling." Figuratively speaking, pastors and
missionaries are viewed as those sitting in the first-class section
while everybody else is back in coach.

The good news is that over the past thirty years, some people who felt this impact of the "Sunday-Monday gap" came together to form what is now known as the faith and work movement, which started from their frustration with the limited relevance of the Christian message to everyday work. These leaders sought to take principles from the Bible and apply them into our *work lives*. In *God at Work*, David Miller notes that common issues include identity, meaning, purpose, calling, discipleship, ethics, responsibility, witness, evangelization, and transformation in and of the business world.[4]

Most of the subsequent materials and teachings on faith and work can be characterized by the following question: How can your faith impact your work? This approach takes faith issues and applies them to our work lives (hereafter referred to as Faith-to-Work model). For example, "pray continually" (1 Thess. 5:17) includes when we are at work and "do not worry about tomorrow" (Matt. 6:34) because God wants us to let him take care of the concerns we tend to shoulder.

Gains follow from this approach. One recent and particularly refreshing look at this Faith-to-Work approach is *Working in the Presence of God* by Denise Daniels and Shannon Vandewarker.[5] These authors offer practical ways for bringing Scripture, commuter liturgy, affirmation, gratitude, confession, and so on, into the "holy ground" of the workplace. We are called to pursue such practices— not just on Sunday, but in all of life.

The Faith-to-Work movement can be characterized as an outside-in approach. We take what is learned from our faith gatherings and carry it forward into Monday to Friday. This model rightfully assumes that truths rooted in the Scriptures have implications for our work week. Figure 1 below illustrates this outside-in approach of seeking to bring learned principles and truths into our work lives. Unfortunately, such truths often don't penetrate far enough into our work lives. This is illustrated by the length of the arrows into the workplace circle in the figure.

In sum, although this Faith-to-Work model offers people some gains, it also places limitations on their union with God. This

Figure 1.1. The Faith → Work Model

approach focuses on the individual worker bringing the right actions and practices into the workplace; but far too often, such practices don't translate into inner transformation and closeness with God, and they can tend to limit our spiritual formation growth. We therefore need to consider the Scriptures more carefully and probe the transformative potential of meeting God in the workplace.

Seeking "Better" Work

The past several decades have brought substantial turbulence into our workplaces. Events such as 9/11 and financial crises brought economic and workforce challenges. Then, in 2020, the COVID-19 pandemic brought a worker shortage and the "Great Resignation" when four million Americans quit their jobs in July 2021, leaving open 10.9 million jobs by the end of that month.[6] These crises often serve as a wake-up call that work is more than just a paycheck and increasing wealth. Business schools have responded to widespread calls to provide research and teaching for the next generation of students with more focus on sustainability, ethics, and social purposes. As a result, many schools have revised their curriculum to integrate moral and ethical values.

Another response has been to think innovatively and address social issues with entrepreneurial ventures.[7] Entrepreneurship can empower purposeful work and provide a pathway for pursuing a given cause by utilizing creativity, innovation, and artistic expression.

Pursuing better work and maintaining work/life balance are good things, and the longing to change the world is God given. But such desires are not sustainable without an inner life rooted in God. The end, however, isn't about becoming more ethical and balanced in our work and life. Life is more than just being passionate and "doing good." The inner strength to engage in such work comes from being able to drink of the living water, as Jesus said, "Whoever drinks the water I give them will never thirst" (John 4:14). The deepest longing of our heart is to be with God and enjoy him now and forever—and I believe that our work context can actually help us move closer to this great desire.

The Potential of Soul Work

In *Christ Plays in Ten Thousand Places*, Eugene Peterson notes that the word *soul* is a comprehensive term for designating the core of who we are, a one-of-a-kind creature made in the "image of God."[8] In Peterson's paraphrase of Genesis 2:7, where God forms man from the ground and then breathe into him, he writes, "The Man came alive—a living soul!" (MSG). "Soul" here speaks to the totality of our God-breathed individuality, our spiritual life, and our relationships with people and the earth.[9]

Since our work is a major part of who we are, to be able to integrate our work with our God-breathed individuality, spirituality, and relationships is to engage with soul work. With such integration comes enormous dignity. To disconnect work from our individuality and spirituality is to reduce it to something mechanical or a function of production. When we separate spirituality from our work, we fracture our lives into something less than what God intended in his breathing life into us. Furthermore, it shortchanges one of the central ways in which God often seeks to touch the core of our lives.

Soul Work therefore probes the realities of having a God-breathed living soul to help us transform our souls in a practical way through our work. Work has the possibility of connecting us to the highest purposes for which we were created; it can become a central facilitator in nourishing our souls, taking us to new heights with God, and thus opening the possibility of gaining immeasurable richness in our lives in God.

What Is Your Core Mindset?

How is your spiritual journey impacted by your work? Which of the following questions most resonate with your challenges?

- Does your workplace seem like a spiritual desert?

- Do you long for after-hours time so you can pursue what you think really matters?

- Do you often feel guilty for not praying, meditating, or even thinking about the Lord when you're at work?

- Are you stuck in a business that provides reasonable earnings, but you don't like what you're doing?

- Do you enjoy your work and being able to help the world become a better place but feel guilty for being so energized by this?

Questions for Reflection

1. What is your core mindset when it comes to faith and work?

2. Do you sense God's presence in your work? If so, how?

3. Do you believe that God is building a bigger story with you through your work?

2

A New Paradigm:
Finding God Already at Work

Almighty God, you are everywhere present and know all things. Open our minds now to better understand how your presence and truths are already immersed in our work. Send your Holy Spirit to engage us in our work in ways that awaken our souls to their deepest desires. We adore and worship you. We want to behold your truth and your glory. Amen.

On the drive home that evening, I suddenly realized that I hadn't once thought about God my entire workday. Sure, I had met him during my quiet time at 6:00 this morning, but what about the last eleven hours? How could I go the whole day without thinking about him?

It was the summer of July 1983, and I was building a two-story home in Ottawa, Kansas. My workdays started at 7:00 a.m., and on this day, we had fitted the rafters into place after having carefully designed and cut each one. We had done a quality job, including the use of wood with excellent structural properties. On my way home, I had a sense of satisfaction with the work we'd completed—but why hadn't I thought about God throughout the process?

The blessed person is one "whose delight is in the law of the LORD, and who meditates on his law day and night" (Ps. 1:2). I have often wondered what the practical application of this psalm could possibly mean for someone like me. After all, building a house requires serious concentration. We were taking exact measurements and making precise cuts with high-speed saws while also thinking two or three steps ahead. How could I possibly add "delights" and "meditations" from Scripture to my day and still do quality work? But I also knew that failing to connect with the Lord for the entire workday was hurting my relationship with him. "How do I practically connect with my Lord while also giving my work the attention it deserves?"

Years later, I still process my workday on the drive home. And years later, I still frequently realize I gave little or no attention to God during those long hours. Sometimes I'd kick myself, wondering how I could have overlooked God the whole day. I'm still learning how I can realistically engage with God when my work demands full concentration.

Since engaging with innovative and excellent work requires full attention, how can we integrate work and faith under such circumstances? The opportunity to share a witness of God is clear. To engage with a project such as bringing safe drinking water to those who are less fortunate is wonderful. To innovate and produce a device that enables disabled veterans is honorable. But what about other ventures, like creating a new food product or developing a new technology for language learning or the development of a solar generator? Are these jobs just as honorable?

As I repeatedly finished my workday feeling dissatisfied for not engaging with God more frequently, I wondered what I was missing. Did my current project hold anything of eternal value? Surely, the Lord had something richer and deeper in mind than what I had just accomplished. Or am I thinking about my work wrongly? Is there something more fundamentally embedded in my work that could connect me with God?

A Stunning Moment

"Have you heard of the book *All Truth Is God's Truth*?"[1] came the question from a colleague at the University of Oklahoma back in 2000. Although I hadn't heard of it, its title stopped me in my tracks. Yes, God is completely true and there is no darkness in him at all—but *all truth*?

Hearing these five words challenged something deeper inside. At the time, I was heavily involved with entrepreneurship research, so truth or the lack thereof was a common part of my everyday work. Did this data accurately address the research question that was asked? Would the findings be skewed if one statistical procedure was used versus another? What were the boundaries of the practical applications?

"All truth is God's truth" is a phrase linked back to St. Augustine (AD 354–430). John Calvin picked it up in his commentary on Titus 1:12, where he states: "All truth is from God; and consequently, if wicked men have said anything that is true and just, we ought not to reject it; for it has come from God."[2] Whatever the source, truth has a unifying effect and will align with what is truthful. As Justin Taylor writes, "Because God's reality is unified and coherent, centered as it is on the person of Christ, all truthful*ness* . . . will cohere and contribute to an integrated, unified, Christ-centered vision of all things."[3]

I knew that the Scriptures were truth, but could my research possibly uncover some aspects of God's truth as well? Maybe research findings are like discovering a small piece of God's truth: "All that I know now is partial and incomplete, but then I will know everything completely, just as God now knows me completely" (1 Cor. 13:12).

Of course, research conducted with human hands and minds will always have limitations, gaps, and errors. But maybe solid findings from research and new innovations are opportunities to peer into some untapped truths of God's universe. While the Scriptures are the rock-solid gold standard, other truths also have their roots in God and can point us to him.

Whether it's discovering how a lateral-flow diagnostic tool can differentiate between the common flu versus a virus, or how corn husks can be reconstituted to make a better tamale wrap, or a software solution allows a shoe store to offer better customer service—all such entrepreneurial pursuits build on elements of God's creation.

If we have the eyes to see, then we should recognize that much of our work builds from the foundational elements of God's creation. For those of us engaging with innovations, it's an honor and a privilege to involve our hands and minds in uncovering pieces of the mystery of God's creation. Discovery of "truth" can be profound because it connects our work with the Creator's handiwork.

The realization that all truth is God's truth is foundational for considering what we do every day. We have the privilege of engaging with our hands and minds with what God has made. Whether our work involves chemicals or liquids from the earth, plant life, or working with individuals, God created us in his image and an abundance of opportunities exists for us to discover his thumbprints in our work and engage with him there.

Why therefore is truth so pivotal for our faith in a work context? Why does God give us the opportunity to learn about and connect with his remarkable truths whether they're from the Scriptures, elements of creation, other humans, or something his Spirit has brought to light in our own minds? The purpose of truth is to stimulate our desires and delights in our God. As John Piper says, "All truth exists to display more of God and awaken more love for God."[4]

Worship is a response to what we have come to learn and know about God (which we will discuss more fully in chapter 9). And since we exist "for the glory of God" (1 Cor. 10:31), God's truth is foundational for bringing to our minds his majesty, beauty, and worth. Truth is substance for our worship. Thus the purpose of connecting with God's truths is to "make God known and loved and shown."[5]

A New Paradigm

As we saw in chapter 1, the Faith-to-Work model is an outside-in approach driven by our faith initiatives. It brings what we learn of our faith from outside of work and seeks to find ways to give it expression in the workplace.

This book develops a new paradigm called "God Already at Work." Since God is already at our work and all truth resides with him, this opens the door for him to touch and speak to us. Work offers multiple pathways for us to connect with God. Because God's truth is already present in our work, it can awaken growth and healing and bring opportunities for us to love God and our neighbors.

Consider this question: How does your work impact your relationship with God? Think about the innovative changes you may be pressing into, the difficulties you're seeking to solve, or the organization you're trying to build. Might God's creation and truths have much to do with these elements?

The God-Already-at-Work paradigm is like a sign pointing us toward our work and how it can become a central catalyst for soul work. Soul work is about connecting with God with our whole being—mind, will, and emotions. Since our specific focus here is on finding God in our work, we should be able to see multiple pathways for opening our desire for God and delighting in him. The truths of God that become evident in our work afford us significant opportunities to engage him and his soul-satisfying presence.

The Faith-to-Work model encourages us to bring the right thoughts and behaviors to work. However, the God-Already-at-Work approach encourages us to look for him already in our work, providing opportunities for his Spirit to come and touch us there. This paradigm takes what we touch, smell, hear, taste, and see as a part of our work and opens the doors of our heart to God. God has always been there and awaits us now!

If you can see the Creator and Sovereign God already involved in your work, then your windows will start to open. Since God is so much bigger than our current spiritual interests, and chapter 4 and following are designed to help you engage with him through your specific work practices.

When the work of our hands links us to our Creator God, amazing channels for connecting with and delighting in the Lord start to open. "Take delight in the LORD, and he will give you the desires of your heart" (Ps. 37:4). Our deepest and most soul-satisfying interests reside with discovering his truths and engaging with his majesty, beauty, and worth. Coming to see God's foundational truths in our work domains is a way of opening us to more of God's "touches" and the transformation of our souls.

The God-Already-at-Work approach (modeled in figure 2.1 below) will underpin our journey throughout this book. By pursuing such pathways as engaging in innovative endeavors, organizing in the Spirit, loving our neighbors, seeking gains from pain, and pursuing justice, we open windows for God's Spirit to come and move among us. When we pursue these pathways, the giver of living water starts to quench our thirst in the often dry and thirsty land of our workplaces, and our spiritual growth and a deeper walk with God is catalyzed by our work.

Opportunities for Connecting with God in the Workplace

Figure 2.1. The "God-Already-at-Work" Model

Getting Inside God's Domain at Work

"What does it mean for those of us serious about our faith to also conduct good research?" This was a question one of my graduate students and I considered one afternoon over coffee in the spring of 2001. After some discussion, the image of a box came to mind. In research, as well as in some work domains, a "black box" is a metaphor for describing a larger system in which there are numerous factors and variables. Some connections between variables may be known, while many others are not. Researchers and practitioners often seek to understand more of these cause-effect relationships and their implications for business.

That afternoon, I drew a picture of a black box on the napkin and labeled it "God's Universe." Of course, God is far too big to be confined to the boundaries of a box; but given the limitations of my little finite mind, images sometimes help to model my thoughts. As a researcher, I've had the privilege of exploring at depth how entrepreneurs make decisions and build businesses to address social needs.

As pictured in figure 2.2 below, research can become a tool to explore elements of God's creation. After moving aside at least some of the dirt and muck, and rightly positioning the lights on the "microscope," I've sometimes observed new insights into what God has created in entrepreneurs, like what stimulates a new innovation or how develop a new highly durable product from recycled plastics. Such discoveries remove a veil from what was previously hidden. When this happens, my heart is stirred and can bring a spirit of awe before my God. Such observations can then turn into worship.

A personalized glimpse into our corner of his creation involves different kinds of wood, soils, plants, plastics, weather conditions, how people learn, and all of it can serve as signposts that point us to God. Consistent with the God-already-at-Work paradigm, we find that insights into God and connecting with him are available in abundance through our work. This can be spiritually transformative. "I'm prepared to contend that the primary location for spiritual formation is the workplace,"[6] writes Eugene Peterson. My own journey collaborates Peterson's statement.

God's Universe

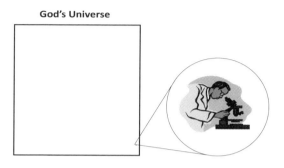

Figure 2.2. The Box of God's Universe

For example, we all have endowments or skills that God makes available to us at multiple levels. The Scriptures sometimes refer to these as "giftings." Numerous tools have been developed to help articulate where we might best make our contributions within the household of faith. Unfortunately, the discussion of our giftings is rarely extended into the workplace. We will take up this topic more fully in chapter 5.

As the creator of all, God longs for us to catch glimpses of him and what he has made. He has given us minds, eyes, noses, ears, and hands to connect with his creation. What our hands find to "touch" in our work can point us to him. God is the creator, and he is everywhere present. If we will just open our eyes, we'll see how our work provides an abundance of glimpses of his thumbprints. These glimpses are opportunities to know God better, love him more, and be shaped by him.

Soul Work

"Why has some of my work been so formative for my soul?" I once asked myself. Some of my most important advances came through innovations and in loving my "neighbor," including the unlovable at my work. Discovering greater truths of God's creation in my work has led me into some of my deepest worship.

As God was nudging me on my journey forward, I wrestled with articulating the developing patterns. What could I constructively do to open my windows wider for the winds of the Spirit to blow into my life? Then one day when I was conversing with Mike, a former pastor and now entrepreneur, it became clear: Opening my windows to God at work is like the pursuit of *spiritual disciplines.*

The classic spiritual disciplines include prayer, Bible reading, meditation, worship, fasting, and solitude, fellowship, and deeds of service. After further considering the nature and boundaries of these spiritual disciplines, the development of a subcategorization known as spiritual work-disciplines became evident to me.

Dallas Willard defines spiritual disciplines as "activities of mind and body purposefully undertaken, to bring our personality and total being into effective cooperation with the divine order."[7] They are practices grounded in Scripture that enable us to move toward God and experience soul growth. Spiritual disciplines are ways of preparing the soils of our soul for the Spirit to come plant his seeds and accomplish his transforming growth within us.[8]

Practicing the disciplines are ways of opening some of our windows to God, a way of inviting God in to touch and transform us. The pursuit of these disciplines creates opportunities for the winds of the Spirit to blow on us, although they never guarantee God's presence. While disciplines are sometimes seen as something we do to earn God's presence, this isn't the case. We can never earn God's presence. The Living Water comes to us only by way of his grace. As modeled in Figure 2.1 above, God is already at work waiting to connect with us there. The work-disciplines developed here seek to open the windows of our soul for the winds of the Spirit to blow.

After years in full-time ministry, Lynn, an entrepreneur in the clothing design space, started a venture with a core value of giving instead of taking. Rather than seeing work as a means to a paycheck, it became a way of developing relationships, investing in the growing capabilities of others at work, and giving financially to others. Lynn gives her employees the opportunity to pursue their own innovative ideas for the marketplace and how to reach the marketplace more effectively. As a result of her business pursuits, Lynn's relationship with God has grown exponentially and she has experienced substantial transformations from her work in the entrepreneurial venture itself.

In the next section (chapters 4–8), we will discuss opportunities for soul work within entrepreneurial pursuits. We will talk about how the disciplines within our innovative pursuits, our individual strengths, loving others, pursuing justice, and dealing with workplace pains can open up our connections to God. When we're empowered by God's Spirit, the work disciplines result in spiritual fruit. It is my prayer that a better understanding of the work disciplines will greatly help you on your journey with God.

God's Work/Our Work

The Bible is written for *all people*. In it, we find substantial teachings involving everyday vocations like taking care of livestock, tending to security, baking, building, composing poetry and music, administering justice, conducting international business, and so on. The Scriptures frequently use vocational work to give us insightful and life-changing opportunities to unite with God. For example, note how Jesus touched the lives of professional fishermen. After fishing all night, he tells them to again "put out into deep water, and let down the nets for a catch" (Luke 5:1–11). Of course, they were extremely successful! Jesus apparently knew that the way for these disciples to gain clearer insight about following him was through their career as fishermen. Likewise, our occupations and vocations are fertile ground for God to touch our hearts and advance our journeys with him. Are you ready to open up your work life to potentially rich gains with the living God who dwells among us?

Questions for Reflection

1. As we see in Genesis, God worked and, even before the fall, Adam and Eve worked in the garden. Since work at its foundation is good, how does this impact the way you view your work?

2. How are your eyes opening to see God and his truths in your workplace?

3

What Does God Think about Work?

Gracious and loving Heavenly Father, bring your light as we examine your Scriptures on the issue of work and the world we live in. "Lead me in your truth and teach me, for you are the God of my salvation; for you I wait all the day long" (Ps. 25:5). By your Holy Spirit, lay a firm understanding of your truths so that we can unashamedly stand on your intentions for our work. Amen.

"Starting Natural Purifiers has been the hardest thing I've ever encountered," said Trevor, the founder of a venture that offers products to disinfect public gathering places. "It has been the right thing to do, and the need is great; businesses and organizations need to be able to purify public meeting spaces. But the challenges with clearing government regulations, resolving a glitch in the applicator, and overcoming user skepticism have all made it a long road."

In pondering his current entrepreneurial journey, Trevor asked me, "Why does everything have to be so hard? What would starting a venture be like if we lived in a world untarnished by greed, false claims, skepticisms, people not remaining true to their word, and threats of litigation? Is the 'curse' responsible for all these problems?"

Questions like these are important but rarely adequately addressed. References from the Bible on work often include Colossians 3:23 ("Whatever you do, work at it with all your heart, as working for the Lord, not for human master") and 1 Corinthians 10:31 ("So whether you eat or drink or whatever you do, do it all for the glory of God"). These certainly are good verses, but the Scriptures offer much more. To understand work and the possible spiritual flourishing therein, we need to align with the foundations given in the Scriptures.

To address this need, in this chapter, we will develop four biblical pillars for thinking more fully about work according to the Scriptures. We will first look at work before and after the curse as recorded for us in Genesis 1–3. This is followed by looking at what else Scripture says about the relevance of creation and work in our lives. Then we consider the Samaritan woman's encounter with the metaphor of Living Water. Finally, we consider parables from the workplace that Jesus used to communicate core truths.

Work before and after the Curse

"Cursed is the ground because of you; through painful toil you will eat food from it all the days of your life" (Gen. 3:17). "By the sweat of your brow you will eat your food until you return to the ground" (Gen. 3:19). These are some of the hard words God pronounces to Adam and Eve after they ate the forbidden fruit.

In considering what the Bible has to say about work, these verses from Genesis 3 are usually among the first to be considered. As a result, "work" is widely seen as painful and necessary because of the curse. Indeed, the "ground" does have many thorns and rocks, which makes our labor challenging.

However, these verses are not the first in the Bible to talk about the idea of work. Starting with Genesis 1:1, we read that "God created the heavens and the earth" and then that God separated the light from the darkness, he gathered the waters so that plant life emerged, and he created animals.

Genesis 2:1–2 sums it up: "Thus the heavens and the earth were completed in all their vast array. By the seventh day God had finished the work he had been doing; so on the seventh day he rested from all his work." God worked for six days in creating the heavens and the earth, and upon the completion of this "work," he then rested. After this, God noted that "there was no one to work the ground" (Gen. 2:5). The work was not yet complete. Consequently, God created human life as stated in 2:7: "The LORD God formed a man from the dust of the ground and breathed into his nostrils the breath of life, and the man became a living being" (Gen. 2:7). In Genesis 2:15, we read: "The LORD God took the man and put him in the Garden of Eden to work it and take care of it." God worked creating the heavens and the earth and it was very good! Then God formed humankind to engage in work, to raise children, to care for the animals, and to work the garden.

As in the Garden of Eden, when we properly tend to and care for the land and animals, we receive many benefits. If we till the soil, plant good seeds, and pull out the weeds, then the opportunity for a productive harvest emerges and we have food to eat.

What amazing insights the book of Genesis provides! As a foundation for our understanding about work, here are some key points from its first three chapters:

- God worked in creating our universe and it was "good."

- God created humankind in his image with the command to work.

- Humankind was commissioned to care for the animals and work the garden.

- After the entry of sin, we still work but now it is significantly harder.

From the beginning, work was good, but then sin threw a wrench into the gears, making work far more difficult. Given our original design, however, there is still much dignity for us when we engage in work. This leads to the following insight.

Biblical Pillar #1: *Work was good from the beginning. The curse made work much more challenging, but there is still good to come from it.*

The Wonders of God's Creation in Our Work

Beyond Genesis 1–3, the Scriptures have much to offer for further understanding of work. Let's start with Job 12:7–10:

> "But ask the animals, and they will teach you, or the birds in the sky, and they will tell you; or speak to the earth, and it will teach you, or let the fish in the sea inform you. Which of all these does not know that the hand of the LORD has done this? In his hand is the life of every creature and the breath of all mankind."

These verses provide us with several notable insights. First, it is again affirmed that the Lord made all of creation from the beginning. This Job passage is particularly intriguing in that saying that the animals, birds, and fish all know "the hand of the LORD."

The created world is waiting to offer us instruction and insights about God, pointing us to his glory. Look at creation for truth about God. Intentionally consider the lilies of the field, listen to the birds of the air who sing to you about God, ponder the ants, the fish of the sea will inform you, and the earth will teach you (Prov. 30:18–19; Matt. 6:26–29; Luke 6:48).

Psalm 19 is also powerful: "The heavens *declare* the glory of God, and the sky above *proclaims* his handiwork. Day to day *pours out speech*, and night to night *reveals knowledge*" (vv. 1–2). The glory of God is in the heavens! Start absorbing its beauty and greatness. One evening of gazing into the heavens can reveal one small measure of their glory. New knowledge is revealed from them every day. One day's speech or observations are far from complete. New revelations continue. Look up and listen to what God might be saying!

There are great insights to be gained from God's creation for our work if we just take the time to observe. We need to open our eyes and take long, thoughtful looks at what God has created and has made accessible to us. Through them, we can gain understanding into who God is. The Scriptures certainly have so much wisdom and insight to offer for knowing God and his desire to prepare us for a glorious eternity with him. Furthermore, creation also offers us additional insights about God. God has imprinted all of creation with who he is.

Of course, many others have recognized these God touches in creation. Centuries ago, Bonaventure (1221–1274) saw all of creation speaking of God by its origin, magnitude, beauty, plenitude, operation, and order.[1] Luther saw creation as "the most beautiful book of the Bible; in it God has described and portrayed Himself."[2] Thus, we have two important books for learning of God: the Scriptures and creation.

So much of our daily work builds from God's creation. Whether you have a business building a more effective tool for bricklayers, implementing air purifiers for disease resistance, engineering a better sound system for the impaired, a software application for more effective math learning, serving food, or applying paint to inhabited space, all legitimate work has its roots in materials and people made by our God.

Consider how the damage from beetle larvae in pine trees creates unique streaks of color in the wood—oranges, greens, grays, and blues. Entrepreneurial furniture designers are finding ways to take beetle-kill pine trees and transform them into beautiful furniture.

As John van Sloten writes in *Every Job a Parable*, "If God's thoughts are embedded in physical nature, could they also be embedded in human nature, the culture we create, the history we live out, and the work we do, even as these things are tainted by sin?"[3] With every job comes the opportunity to uncover the thumbprints of God. We can learn to appreciate God and his handiwork in sunrises, the sprouting of seeds, the amount of sun and heat different plants require, mountains, waterfalls, and seasonal variations.

Biblical Pillar #2: *All nature, including that which is embedded in our work, shows us God, since all of creation reflects his imprints.*

Work Saved This Woman's Life

A third biblical pillar is based on how Jesus connects with people in their place of work. He often uses similes and metaphors to make understandable a perfect truth. Jesus' encounter with the Samaritan woman is such a case. Meeting her at the well, he uses water as a metaphor for getting "living water." While this encounter is rarely examined from a work perspective, doing so offers us some important insights. Here is the story as given to us in John 4:6–16.

> Jacob's well was there, and Jesus, tired as he was from the journey, sat down by the well. It was about noon.
>
> When a Samaritan woman came to draw water, Jesus said to her, "Will you give me a drink?" (His disciples had gone into the town to buy food.)
>
> The Samaritan woman said to him, "You are a Jew and I am a Samaritan woman. How can you ask me for a drink?" (For Jews do not associate with Samaritans.)
>
> Jesus answered her, "If you knew the gift of God and who it is that asks you for a drink, you would have asked him and he would have given you living water."
>
> "Sir," the woman said, "you have nothing to draw with and the well is deep. Where can you get this living water? Are you greater than our father Jacob, who gave us the well and drank from it himself, as did also his sons and his livestock?"
>
> Jesus answered, "Everyone who drinks this water will be thirsty again, but whoever drinks the water I give them will never thirst. Indeed, the water I give them will become in them a spring of water welling up to eternal life."
>
> The woman said to him, "Sir, give me this water so that I won't get thirsty and have to keep coming here to draw water."
>
> He told her, "Go, call your husband and come back."

First, Jesus makes the connection with the Samaritan woman through her work. She is going about her job as a water-gatherer, most likely a daily chore. Jesus initiates the conversation with her through this job by asking her for a drink. The woman appears quite reluctant, probably due to cultural and personal reasons. However, she could understand Jesus' need because they both felt the heat of the day. Jesus utilizes this moment to engage her through her work—and it turns out to be a life-changing conversation, not only just for her but for her entire village.

I doubt she would have responded to Jesus in one of her other domains. Her home and social context would likely have been completely closed to him. However, her work as a water-gatherer surfaced a small opening in her door for Jesus to access. Jesus seems to have a way of finding those opportune moments to personally show us he is the true source of life. The workplace is one of those places, as it is where so many of our deeper realities and vulnerabilities emerge.

Second, Jesus connects to the spiritual longing of the Samaritan woman through the central object of water in the heat of the day. Jesus extends from water in her work domain to metaphorically address the concept of "living water." He knew that the thirst of her spiritual soul is greater than her physical thirst, and he offers her that deeply satisfying living water, which will provide a quenching and unspeakable joy for all eternity.

Living water comes as a gift for those who ask Jesus. Given the thirst of our souls, we want to drink deeply of this soul-satisfying living water. Our souls will die of thirst if it does not drink from the right source. Drinking of Jesus and his living water satisfies forever.

The various wandering of the Samaritan woman had left her soul parched, but it also led to her eager receptivity to the living water Jesus offered. Her work context in the heat of the day gave Jesus the opportune moment to engage her, and with this water metaphor, Jesus "hit the spot" and therefore enabled this woman to understand her deepest need. This moment at the well changed her life for all eternity!

Biblical Pillar #3: *Jesus meets us in our work context where our deeper realities often surface. He often uses metaphors and similes from our work to get us to the truth.*

Mind-Bending Learning with Jesus at Work

The fourth biblical pillar for God in the workplace is revealed in Jesus' great interest in our work. He was a master storyteller and built many of his parables around labor contexts such as lost sheep, wheat and weeds, and vineyard workers. For him, parables were earthy stories common to everyday life that convey a spiritual truth. Although many of those listening to him wanted a recipe or checklist to follow, or at least to consider, Jesus was going in another direction and masterfully used parables to communicate his point.

Although our spiritual journeys naturally have much to gain by considering these parables, our work journeys also have much to gain by considering them as *work* parables with spiritual meaning. There are at least four reasons why Jesus' parables are so vital to us.

First, most of Jesus' parables directly connect us with the workplace. Of course, the Gospel writers focused mostly on Jesus' ministry years, but we can surmise from Scripture that before those three years, he worked as a craftsman in the construction industry, possibly even as head of the family business for the last years. His teachings along with most of the parables show him to be knowledgeable and interested in business dealings.

Jesus seemed to love being with workers in the workplace, where everyday life was happening. A closer look at the thirty-seven parables in the Gospels of Matthew, Mark, and Luke show significant attention to this. Of these thirty-seven parables, thirty-two (86 percent) utilize distinct work activities. In twenty-five (68 percent) of them, Jesus builds the story line around a labor context.[4] This includes the purchase of real estate, one who sows seeds, and faithful and unfaithful managers, to name a few.

Although we can't know for sure, it's interesting to think about what Jesus actually did for work before he started his full-time ministry. The Gospels say he worked as a "carpenter" (see Mark 6:3 and Matt. 13:55). In that case, perhaps Jesus had to work in challenging work conditions with weather delays, coordination with other contractors and tradesmen, and issues with getting paid. Perhaps the ups and downs of the business workday were a regular part of his life. Through all this, he knew that he could use the workplace as an important way of connecting with those around him—and even us today.

Second, Jesus' parables show that he saw the workplace as a learning hub. He often built the story lines of his parables around important aspects of lending money, thievery, planting crops, vineyard workers, shepherding, and construction. In so doing, he associated with a familiar part of many of his listeners' lives. Jesus' parables tell a clear story starting with a workplace truth with which his audience could quickly connect.

More importantly, Jesus showed the kingdom of heaven to be intertwined with the workplace. By teaching with parables, Jesus enabled those around him to learn about the kingdom of heaven by presenting them with workplace realities. Instead of teaching only on the Sabbath, Jesus connected the workplace with meaning about the kingdom of heaven.

Third, through his parables, Jesus used the workplace to help facilitate deeper learning. He combined experiences from everyday life to illustrate a profound truth. It was if Jesus was applying the 80/20 rule from the "Pareto principle to learning."[5] This principle states that if we are already familiar with at least 80 percent of what is being discussed, then we are much more receptive to learning about the remaining 20 percent. Once the 20 percent level of new content is reached, then our human retention level starts missing bigger chunks of what is being communicated.

With Jesus' parables, however, his listeners were likely above the 80 percent familiar threshold. That is, they understood that a seed dies before it germinates and gives life to a new plant or that a single lost sheep must be sought or lost forever. After setting the story line with which they were familiar, Jesus then often inserted an unexpected turn or surprise. For example, in the parable of the two debtors with one having 500 denarii and the other 50 denarii forgiven, Jesus asks, "Now which of them will love him [the money-lender] more?" (Luke 7:41–42).

This illustrates where the deeper lessons of the parable often get established. With a few words, Jesus exposes hardness of heart, confronts prejudices, and brings about conviction. His listeners often left amazed, speechless, perplexed, and challenged. Some even put their heads together, seeking to ascertain the point Jesus was trying to make. For Jesus, the workplace represented a context for deep learning.

People learn when they can move from what they understand to what they do not understand. Furthermore, when we can connect our workplace with a spiritual truth, as with Jesus' parables, deep learning can occur. As we proceed with the work of our hands, further thoughts and entrenchment are likely come. With such learning, Jesus beautifully transforms our understanding of what it means to know our God who is already at our work!

Biblical Pillar #4: *Jesus frequently used parables set in work contexts to take us into deeper learning of his perfect truth.*

A Firm Foundation

Most of us struggle to understand the spiritual side of work. With the four pillars offered above for the great value of work, however, you are now in a position to take advantage of the mighty rock on which you can stand. Work no longer needs to be seen as something we endure so we can get to the spiritual dimension of our lives. With God, work can truly become transformational.

We have seen how work was God's idea in the very beginning of creation. Then being made in his image, he invited us to join him in tilling the soil and tending to the animals. He established the universe, and the creation process is still ongoing. He invited us to become co-creators with him. Yes, because of sin, we do work in pain and by the sweat of our brow, but work is still ordained by God.

Through everything God has made, we can see his thumbprints. We now have the privilege of coming face-to-face and finger-to-finger with God in what we hear, see, taste, smell, and touch through our work. In this way, God the Creator of all things comes near. He then sets us about in our work to be involved with his creation and our efforts as co-creators in the raw materials, the environment, animals, water, plants, oxygen, the people with whom we work, and so on.

God longs to connect with us, and he often and maybe frequently initiates with us in our work as he did the Samaritan woman in her work as a water-gatherer. Jesus seemed to consider that much of work can be a powerful reflector of his kingdom, which is probably why he based most of his parables on the realities in the workplace.

At its core, our work involves the created order that God has put into place. Our work can be full of major touch points with our God. God is already there in our work, desiring to touch the core of our soul. As John Calvin saw it, the world is a theater of God's glory.[6] Entrepreneurial and workplace endeavors provide us with amazing opportunities to learn about him and to stand in awe of what he is doing. *Immanuel*—God is with us! (Matt. 1:23).

In the next five chapters, we will develop the work disciplines for discovering the truth and presence of God already at our work in (1) the innovations with which we engage, (2) our giftedness, (3) the "neighbors" with whom we toil, (4) the pursuit of workplace justice, and (5) encountering trials in the workplace. It is my hope that these five chapters will be like a pathway that moves you closer to God in your work.

Consider again the central question of this book: *How is your work impacting your relationship with God?* Is your work serving as a means for deepening your discoveries of God? I trust you now see the firm foundation on which you can stand for getting to soul-quenching work.

Questions for Reflection:

1. Which of the four pillars for a biblical foundation for work resonates most with you? Why?

2. Where is God's creation and his imprints already most evident to you in your work?

3. What metaphors and parables in your work do you think God may be giving you to teach you about his kingdom?

PART II

OPPORTUNITIES FOR EXPERIENCING GOD AT WORK

4

ENGAGING GOD THROUGH INNOVATION

Creator God, thank you that you have made the huge galax-
ies and the smallest micro cells of our bodies and everything
in between. We honor and praise your holy name for all of
your creation. With the abilities given, you have also commis-
sioned us to co-create. Come now and open our eyes as we
innovate with you. We desire to see you more clearly and to
touch your thumbprints already embedded in creation. Amen.

"The more I come to understand the properties of spider silk as a
key component in a composite material we're developing for making
backpacks," said Samuel, "the more awed I become with God and
the intricacies of his creation. The properties of spider silk, including its strength and elasticity and extreme lightweight, are amazing."

Samuel is a part of a startup team working on super-lightweight
yet durable backpacks. Most backpacks on the market start at six
pounds and are notorious for sacrificing comfort, durability, and
functionality. Research from the University of Bristol School of
Chemistry shows spider silk to be five times stronger than steel of
the same diameter.[1] Such realities are examples of God's truth. For
backpackers, spider silk combined with carbon fiber threads and
nylon can be of great value by easing their carrying load.

Experiences like Samuel's spider silk are widespread in the
world of entrepreneurship. Maybe you need just the right kind sand
to build water filters. Or perhaps you are using sand with high levels
of quartz for making semiconductors, or you need a fine and uni-
form sand for propping open fractured rocks. There are hundreds
of different kinds of sand and many more uses.

Whether your innovation uses plant matter, chemicals, or sand or spider webs, we know who the Creator is. Innovations can point us to God and to aspects of God's truth and the intricacies and beauty of what he has made. This can be an important stepping stone for meaningful soul work.

Entrepreneurship in God's Creation

Engaging in innovations is like having a front-row seat in the theater of God. The opportunities to behold his greatness in the innovations we pursue are endless. But this amazing creation of God recorded in Genesis 1 is only the beginning. In Genesis 1:27, we read that "God created man in his own image, in the image of God he created him; male and female he created them." Being made in God's image means we have the mind and capabilities to carry forward additional work.

Being created in his image involves a "call" to participate with him as co-creators. The instructions God provided for us are as follows.

- "Prosper! Reproduce! Fill Earth! Take charge!" (Gen. 1:28 MSG).

- "Be responsible for fish in the sea and birds in the air, for every living thing that moves on the face of Earth" (Gen. 1:28 MSG).

- "I've given you every sort of seed-bearing plant on earth and every kind of fruit-bearing tree. . . . I give whatever grows out of the ground for food" (Gen. 1:29 MSG).

God clearly is the Creator. He is the only One who can and has created from nothing. He is the One who put the initial building blocks into place. And we now have the opportunity and mandate to build and fill the earth, provide food for one another, and fill our culture with good things. We get the opportunity to co-create together with him!

While Genesis 1:28 is usually applied to reproduction, Tim Keller notes that "it means civilization, not just procreation. . . . God does not just want more individuals of the human species; he also wants the world to be filled with a human society."[2] God is entrusting us with the ability to come alongside him and be co-creators. He has embedded creative characteristics in each of us, not unlike what he used to carry out the creation process recorded for us in Genesis 1!

Jordan Raynor also notes that God left much of creation as incomplete for follow-on co-creators to pursue.[3] God created fish, but he did not inform us how to catch fish. He created horses, but they don't arrive as trained animals beneficial for humankind. God provided seeds for crops like corn, carrots, coconuts, and cotton, but he didn't say how to cultivate them. He didn't tell us how climate conditions impact the yields or how to turn cotton into clothing. He made the earth with oil reservoirs far beneath the surface, but he didn't tell us where those reservoirs are located or how to extract the oil or how to refine crude oil into gasoline along with now literally thousands of other products. When illnesses and wounds inflict us, various minerals and plant elements can be combined and processed with the aid of various technologies to create medicines for healing.

God created humankind to carry the "mantle" forward, to take the raw materials of land, trees, plants, and animals to build and extend what has been given. It became humankind's responsibility to "work the ground" (Gen. 2:5) and take the garden of Eden and "work it and take care of it" (Gen. 2:15). Stated differently, we are to help build better societies.

Only humans are endowed with the ability and mission of multiplying the created work that God started. It is the responsibility of humans to build good societies and set up helpful institutions, to be entrepreneurial stewards of the resources that God has provided. From these resources, we have the privilege of turning them into goods and services that contribute to the common good.

How intriguing it is, then, that after the Lord God formed every living creature, "he brought them to the man to see what he would name them" (Gen. 2:19). Humankind's God-given creativity was quickly put into action by naming every living creature. How intriguing that even God was interested in learning what names humankind would give to each animal.

What an honor and privilege to be given the co-creating assignment by our God. God is the first and true Creator—the ultimate Maker, the "originator of the origins."[4] He provides the raw materials, and we bring our creative endowments to accomplish fruitfulness! We were designed for work—and when we co-create, we can experience aspects of his calling. What an astonishing privilege!

The Soul Work of Creating

Most of us love to create. This is how God designed us. When we personally engage in innovative endeavors, it touches something deeper within us. As Dorothy Sayers observed, "The characteristic common to God and man is apparently . . . the desire and the ability to make things."[5]

The pattern is set and being human means we have a bent toward creativity. Makoto Fujimura takes this idea further by noting that "our journey to 'know' God requires not just ideas and information, but actual making, to translate our ideas into real objects and physical movements."[6] We have a bent to engage in creativity, but most of all, for learning more of God in what we create.

While Fujimura addresses the artist specifically, this is just as true for entrepreneurs. When we engage in innovations and seek to alter the way something works, the depths of God and his creation start to open. The co-creating process seems to avail us to "God touches"—that is, pieces of God's grace that touch our lives as his thumbprints become more evident.

Engaging with entrepreneurship is a pathway to God! When we're working on an innovation, the windows to deeper learning with God often open. Such learning and crafting from elements of his creation connects us with his very thumbprints. Therefore, co-creating is engaging and instructive and exhilarating. It is what we were made to do, and it gives us insight into the very nature of God.

When we innovate, we become active participants with God in our world. Furthermore, by innovating we open a major pathway for growing our oneness with God.

Going Deeper with the Innovation Process

Recall the image offered in chapter 2 (fig. 2.2) of the researcher looking into a microscope to examine a specific element from the "box" of God's universe. When Samuel works with spider silk's feather-light elasticity and strength, he is gazing into the "microscope" with amazement to the Creator.

For IT people who measure traffic on a website, their observations can be largely mechanical, or they be inquisitive about the human behavior behind the various responses. In analyzing the pathways that website visitors take, they can determine which pathways lead to inquiries and even purchases. Question can also probe how website visitors' behavior changes when graphics and schemes are altered. Or consider a coffee shop owner who decides to study customer satisfaction and buyer behavior. How does a greeting with no smile versus a welcoming smile impact the behavior of customer?

When I was researching decision-making styles, I examined how entrepreneurs differed from managers in large organizations.[7] The more I learned, the more I came to understand important nuances and differences. There are clear benefits for entrepreneurs who extensively use decision rules or shortcuts (sometimes referred to as heuristics) to navigate through the uncertainties of a startup venture. Such decision-making enables entrepreneurs to move forward long before the "hard" evidence becomes available.

While I may be considered an "expert" in entrepreneurial decision-making by some, I often sense that I'm still only at the tip of the iceberg on this phenomenon. Although I have answered questions about whether entrepreneurs use decision rules or heuristics more extensively than managers in large organizations, my

answers always seem to lead to two or three more questions. Sometimes, it's like God is saying, "Yes, and I will go deeper with you.
Here is another piece or two of the puzzle for you to unwrap. I will
walk this journey with you and perhaps give you further insights."

There are at least two reasons why it can be beneficial to further
expand our understanding of the "spider silk" of our domains. First,
the deeper we go, the more we see the thumbprints of God in his
work as Creator. When this happens, we get to stand in awe of who
he is as reflected in what he has made. We get to see more truth!

Second, innovation almost always encourages further development of expertise. To say it another way, the best way to understand
something is to innovate on it. We most likely can't change C without knowing how A and B interact to make C. Although innovation
isn't just creativity, it almost always involves much learning.

Opportunities for Soul Work in Innovation

To guide us with the practical, let's put the innovation process
into segments. Successful innovations usually comprise the four
main components of (1) identifying customer need, (2) personal
mission/passion, (3) knowledge and expertise, and (4) venture
development.

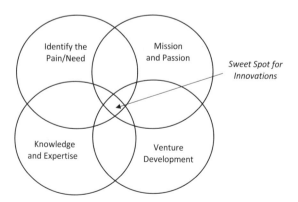

Figure 4.1. Key Components of Innovations

With each component are opportunities for discovering God's imprint in the innovation process. Each is like a "mini" window into discovering God already in our work in our co-creating. Each represents potential entry points for experiencing the thumbprints of God on our lives. Guided by the God-Already-at-Work model, we can look inside innovative work to discover more God's truths and to experience more of his "touches."

Let's now peel back some layers of this innovation onion so we can see more of God and his truths and how we might look for God in different innovation stages.

Identifying the Need

An early step in pursuing an entrepreneurial venture is identifying a viable customer need. Forty-two percent of new ventures fail because of inadequate market needs.[8] An entrepreneurial solution without a specific problem being felt by prospective customers is a path to nowhere. To practice the discipline of innovation on a pathway to connecting with God, consider the following:

- Listen to the real needs of people in your target market. Find ways to engage in deep conversations with them. These are real people with real needs. Does your innovation align with the problem currently being felt by prospective customers?

- Build powerful listening habits. These will inevitably lead you to fresh and innovative ideas.

- Have you talked with God about this innovation? He might have some insights for you.

Mission and Passion

Many entrepreneurs pursue an innovation stemming from a painful life event or a deep concern for a given people group. Passion is critical for all startups because of the perseverance it generates. No new venture can get through the ups and downs of the startup cycle without a sense of mission. It's also valuable for attracting prospective stakeholders and customers. Consider these questions for finding God in your mission and passions:

- Has God given you a passion for a particular people group?
- Has God implanted a special interest in one or more raw materials from his creation?
- Is there a specific unmet need that seems relevant for a given people group?

Knowledge and Expertise

Of the "raw materials" with which you're interested in innovating, around which ones have you developed knowledge and expertise? Innovation invariably involves extending and combining to create something new. Without one or several expertise, challenges that emerge with the innovation are unlikely to be resolvable. Combining expertise with a desire for learning and breaking new ground is ideal. Here are questions for you to consider:

- What knowledge, skills, and understanding has God given you?
- Where might God be inviting you to go deeper into the treasure trove of his creation?
- What truths of his creation are you learning?
- What raw material or phenomenon might you probe more deeply, thus creating channels for seeing more of God's thumbprints and possibly leading to more innovative opportunities?

Venture Development

Moving from a legitimate innovative idea to a viable venture is usually a big step. This process is sometimes referred to as "design thinking" or the "d-school" that was first developed at Stanford.[9] This process is about deep consideration of the needs of a target market with the technical alternatives of the product being offered. Venture development also involves assembling resources that involve equipment, personnel, real estate, and capital. The ability to assemble the needed resources effectively and economically is a part of most successful startups. Here are some questions to consider:

- What resources does your startup venture need? What human capital and resources do you have that God can use?

- What do you not know that you do not know? Pray and seek God for further insights.

- What "Minimum Viable Product" (a basic version of your product to test with potential customers) can you develop? Ask God for insights about your product and your market ahead of the full market roll-out. Look for his provisions.

While all four innovation components are a part of most successful innovations, you may personally feel stronger in one than another. It may well be that only one or two will be relevant to you for going forward with God the Creator. From a perspective of connecting with God, it's likely that only one or two of these components will emerge as effective in nurturing your soul work. Engage and fine-tune your "sweet spot" for discovering God in your innovative pursuits.

Parables of the Hidden Treasure and the Pearl of Great Value

To complete the core chapters (4–8) of this book, I will engage a work parable to put the crown on this chapter. These work parables, which can readily be viewed through an entrepreneurial lens, help us to see how God's truths are relevant for Jesus' day as well as our modern-day entrepreneurs.

Here, I will highlight two closely aligned parables: Jesus' parables of the hidden treasure and the flawless pearl:

> "The kingdom of heaven is like treasure hidden in a field, which a man found and covered up. Then in his joy he goes and sells all that he has and buys that field. Again, the kingdom of heaven is like a merchant in search of fine pearls, who, on finding one pearl of great value, went and sold all that he had and bought it." (Matt. 13:44–46)

In these two parables, the kingdom of heaven is the reign of God; it is a place of salvation and redemption.

In the parable of the hidden treasure, valuable possessions were frequently buried for safekeeping. After the man discovers this treasure in a field, he *gladly* sells all his assets to buy it and thus the treasure. The treasure is equated to the kingdom of heaven. It is worth so much that it is worth every penny the man can muster. It is worth an all-out effort. Seeking the kingdom of heaven and the salvation that it offers is an extraordinary value. With it comes forgiveness of our sins, forever life with God, peace, and joy in knowing God himself.

The life of an entrepreneur is a modern-day parallel to this man in that they give everything for the future of their business. Upon discovering a great business concept, they sell or mortgage their home, downscale their vehicle, work long hours, and dedicate themselves to learning new skills needed for the venture. The opportunity to gain ownership of a priceless treasure (a prime piece of real estate, a strategic alliance with a critical player, a big product sale, and so on) is rare and the payoff can multiply the investment ten, fifty, even a hundredfold. Come and invest all you have!

Here is my entrepreneurial paraphrase of this parable:

> The kingdom of heaven is like an entrepreneur who discovered an excellent opportunity for a new business. Upon learning of the opportunity, he kept this concept secret while he happily

sold his house, downscaled his car, and used all of his savings to buy what he needed for building this venture.

The second parable involving a "pearl of great value" is also about investing in the kingdom of heaven. It closely resembles the parable of the hidden treasure, but with a couple of subtle differences. Whereas the man finding the treasure starts a new business, the pearl is discovered by an entrepreneurial merchant. His search is strategic and ongoing.

Consider this entrepreneurial paraphrase:

> The kingdom of heaven is like an entrepreneur who had long been working to create a new business to solve an important security issue. When the strategic initiative finally reached a viable solution, the entrepreneur knew that the product would be readily accepted. Thus she went and sold her house, car, jewelry, and used all of her savings to buy what she needed to capitalize this venture.

Entrepreneurs are modern-day examples of what it means to give up everything to pursue their business of the hidden treasure or the flawless pearl. The kingdom of heaven is worth every ounce of energy you can put into it. Go and invest heavily in the kingdom of heaven!

In his parables, Jesus says nothing about these two entrepreneurs having to sell all they have, including their business. Rather, he uses their businesses as a means of penetrating a key truth about following him. What additional parable and learning do you think God wants to teach you through your business? God will be honored by your pursuits as you uncover truths in your work about following him.

Your entrepreneurial endeavors are vital channels for the growing of the kingdom of heaven within you. Invest! Ask the Holy Spirit to open your eyes to see more truth. The Father longs to meet you in your work. He will greatly reward such endeavors.

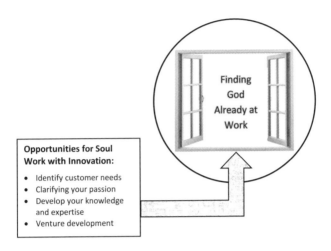

Opportunities for Soul
Work with Innovation:

- Identify customer needs
- Clarifying your passion
- Develop your knowledge
  and expertise
- Venture development

Finding
God
Already at
Work

Chapter Model and Summary
Figure 4.2. Innovating for Soul Work

Engaging with innovation is a unique and wonderful opportunity to learn about God and connect with him for some remarkable soul work. Probing the depths of an innovation and gazing into his thumbprints can take you into some special understanding of his world. Articulating the needs of prospective customers or bringing to fruition a special passion God that implanted in you or using your expertise to innovatively link some dots previously never connected, or your ability to assemble and organize resources for a new startup can offer significant soul advancement potential. Engaging with innovation and these four components can provide you with multiple opportunities to discover and absorb God's truth.

There is nothing more valuable and precious than seeking of the kingdom of God. Use the innovation process to find God's thumbprints. He is already present. Invest all you have to find him there so you can enjoy him!

Your Next Step

1. What innovation(s) have you been involved with that gave you insight into the depths of God and his creation? Thank God for the insights you have gained.

2. What component of the innovation process are you best at? In what part might you ask God for further growth so that you can find more of him in your work?

5

PRACTICING YOUR SPIRITUAL GIFTS AT WORK

Almighty God, "You knit me together in my mother's womb"
(Ps. 139:13). You continue to craft me after your image.
Thank you for the opportunities to extend them to others
for your glory. Grow my relationship with you through the
utilization and continual development of your gifts to me so
they may multiply your redeeming purpose in Jesus Christ
our Lord. Amen.

"Eric is a good employee with reasonable versatility, but he has trouble finishing the tasks put in front of him," said the owner of the building supply store. "When I ask him to sort through a pile of lumber or to load a truck with building supplies, he proceeds but easily gets distracted. By 3:00 p.m., he's watching the clock in anticipation of the end of the workday."

After years of employment, one day Eric decided to follow his dream and become an entrepreneur. He was bored by his job at the building supply store. His skill set was not deepening, he was becoming apathetic about life, and he was having little or no positive impact on the lives of those around him.

Eric's life changed in becoming an entrepreneur. He became invigorated by the process of repurposing an existing building for a food service company, developing the needed supply chain, and acquiring quality equipment at a reasonable price, among other things. Instead of feeling mentally and physically exhausted when he came home from work, Eric now has more energy. While being an entrepreneur is keeping him more than busy, he is more positive and more involved with family life. He also has renewed spiritual interest. Eric's pathway into entrepreneurship and his increased growth as a person is one of the reasons I enjoy hanging out with these type of people.

Meaningful work is so rewarding when it happens, but far too often, work is little more than a means to an end—a paycheck so we can live. In addressing meaningful work, Jordan Raynor says that many of us "are overcommitted, overwhelmed, and overstressed, spending way too much time focused on minutiae rather than the work we believe God created us to do."[1] Without becoming an outstanding performer in a specific trade or work skill, we tend to relegate ourselves to the world of mediocrity and ordinariness. Such work does little to help us serve others and grow spiritually.[2]

A friend once likened the development of our career paths to motorboats and sailboats. Some people are like motorboats: they know the career they want to pursue when they're still in their teen years and set off on a reasonably straight path in their chosen career. The career path for most of us, however, is more like a sailboat that goes back and forth, hopefully making progress with finding a good fit with our jobs.

Each job, including those in the gig economy, have the potential to further inform us about our strengths and weaknesses and insights into the kind of work we are best fit for. Unfortunately, some of us overlook such learning opportunities and let ourselves get mired in the day-to-day. These types of career paths even seem to distance us from deeper growth with God as well. So how do we move beyond being an "average" performer to get to soul-satisfying work?

Take Your "Giftings" to Work!

Entrepreneurs are intriguing individuals. Some are skilled with developing innovative solutions, while others are excellent at gathering resources or designing new organizations. Still others can get to a working solution by improvising almost anything or have an outstanding aptitude for making strategic investments.

Coming beside entrepreneurs is like seeing glimpses of God's creation and his making of "entrepreneurs" in his image. Privately though, I have long wondered how relevant the concept of spiritual gifts might be for the workplace. Is this stretching the application of the Scriptures too far?

Two issues have long given me pause me when spiritual gifts are discussed. Since we rarely hear about spiritual gifts being applied to the workplace, it makes us wonder if they're for use only in the household of faith. Then I recall individuals I've known who work in agriculture, new business startups, language learning via software, innovating a new maintenance firm, and many other ventures. I then wonder how we can we make sense of some of these amazing capabilities that we observe in the workplace.

The other issue adding to my confusion is the distinction between "spiritual gifts" and "talents." Some claim that our talents are genetic and are therefore something we're born with,[3] while we receive our spiritual gifts from the Holy Spirit after we come into a relationship with Jesus.

Of course, the topic of spiritual gifts has attracted its share of attention in Christian circles. Although it's beyond the scope of this book to unwrap the numerous nuances, there are important insights for their use in the workplace.

First, spiritual gifts clearly reach beyond the boundaries of the church because they're meant for the common good of all. For example, by definition, the gift of evangelism extends beyond the household of faith. Also, Jesus healed many people who weren't then in a faith community, and we can make similar extensions with other gifts such as mercy and service.

Second, abilities, time, family relationships, insights, wisdom, money, and skills (collectively referred to here as gifts, talents, and/ or resources) exist because they're a part of the creation that God designed and sourced to us. In following Jesus, our gifts, talents, and resources are for use now and into our life eternal (Matt. 25:14–30).

In view of the new creation, Albert Wolters notes that "all human talents and abilities can flourish and blossom under the regenerating and sanctifying influence of the Holy Spirit to the glory of service of God. When opened by the Spirit they are all charismatic gifts."[4] Our interest is in giving God honor and glory as for what he imparts to us by way of gifts, talents, resources, and much more.

For the sake of brevity, I have summarized below some biblical truths on giftedness, talents, and resources that are relevant for our workplace discussion:

- Gifts, talents, time, wisdom, relationships, resources, etc., have their origin in God.

- All human beings are made in God's image and reflect his majesty, beauty, and worth through the talents and resources he has given us.

- To become more Godlike is to grow toward wholeness in all of life. This includes the utilization of the resources God has given throughout our lives.

- With our spiritual birth, the Holy Spirit gives us spiritual insights and words to extend the glory of God to others.

- Spiritual gifts involve illuminating our God-given talents and abilities to specifically reflect the majesty, beauty, and worth of God to others.[5]

- Spiritual gifts extend beyond the household of faith and rightly include the workplace.

- All gifts, talents, and resources give us windows into seeing God more clearly. They also provide us with pathways to unite with God more closely.

- We radiate God's presence most clearly to others when we channel him through the gifts and talents he has given us.

- The receiving of gifts and talents doesn't imply they are fully formed. Rather, they typically involve development, training, and fine-tuning to increase their worth.

With these truths, we can now delve further into the realities of the entrepreneurship world.

Burnout and Failure

Work burnout is a big problem for founders as well as employees, and most people experience it at some point in their lives. During the time of the COVID-19 global pandemic in 2021, numbers indicate that approximately 50 percent of the workforce were feeling burned out at any given point in time.[6] Instead of feeling vigorous, engaged, and effective, they were chronically fatigued and became uninvolved and unproductive.

Building a company is one of the most challenging adventures someone could undertake. Entrepreneurs deal with limited resources, product failure, key employee turnover, broken promises, and unanticipated competition. As they get pushed beyond their limits in the face of so much uncertainty, it's common for them to feel burnout and anxiety over the very real possibility of failure.

Although burnout happens for several reasons, a major culprit is a long-term mismatch between who we are as individuals and our work or work context. With all the challenges of entrepreneurship—such as unexpected delays, disappointing returns, broken promises, unanticipated problems, and global pandemics—there are multiple opportunities for our personal limitations to show themselves. Entrepreneurs must often be a Jack of all trades.

There is also the reality that as humans, we can only do so much. When the majority of our work has us operating outside of our giftedness zone for a long season, burnout is inevitable. This is where we need to ask questions about our work-life balance, exercise, and eating well.

Not enough attention, however, is given to the role of our giftedness. After a startup season where entrepreneurs are required to wear many hats, they need to make an effort then to narrow the scope of their work and then build their organization around their strengths and giftedness. Instead, they often focus on trying to shore up their weaknesses so they can at least get to par. This is a tough route to go and one that will inevitably lead to burnout. You need to know your strengths. Stop trying to be a Jack or Jill of all trades and a master of none. What matters the most for your business and your career is that you can focus on and excel in your unique gifting.[7]

Finding your God-given giftings and talents is often a bit of a journey. Jordan Raynor notes three questions to ask yourself to identify your strengths:[8]

- What am I passionate about?
- What gifts has God given me?
- Where do I have the best opportunity to glorify God in serving others?

It's the combination of these three filters where you'll find your strengths, gifts, and talents. But you need to ask yourself all three questions as looking at just one can likely lead you to misdiagnose yourself.

The workplace may well be the best place to understand and use your giftedness. To reserve your giftedness only for the household of faith is to draw a line between the secular and the sacred. Jesus told us to love our neighbors and those who persecute us, not just those at church. Our God-given giftedness is relevant to all of life.

Raynor recounts the time one of his mentors asked him, "What is the one thing you want to really sink your teeth into?" In his helpful book *Called to Create*, he effectively encourages us to become a master of one area so we can engage in more effective service to God and others.[9]

We drastically shortchange the potential fruitfulness of our lives if we don't develop and utilize our God-given gifts in the workplace. This active pursuit does involve its own discipline, but this is a way to open up the possibility of experiencing the beauty and intricacies of how the Maker has designed us. In the following section, we will discuss a pathway for pursuing our giftedness.

Opportunities for Soul Work with Your Giftings

As I already mentioned, our journey to finding our giftedness is often more like the sailboat journey. We travel back and forth with incremental gains in our understandings, but it's still a pathway worth taking. If we don't advance in this path, Tim Keller notes that we'll never get to love others through our "ministry of competency."[10] Meaningful joy comes to both the giver and the receiver when our gifts and talents are utilized. But with offering a ministry of competence comes perseverance and a lifetime of learning. Let's now consider opportunities in our workplaces to make strides with our ministry of competence.

The Discipline of Action

If our giftings and resources are to be a vital part in our lives, then they need continual development. Taking action is constructive and even imperative for sharpening our key resources. Although I may sense that I have the talent of improvising new innovations or bootstrapping resources, only as I act will I come to understand the boundaries and nuances.

As you take action, pay close attention to both solicited and unsolicited feedback. Where and when are people and organizations most impacted by your giftings? What talents and skills most impact the quality of your work?

The Discipline of Competency

Focus is a particular challenge for entrepreneurs. Launching a new venture requires versatility in multiple areas with limited resources, but this doesn't exempt you from the pursuit of becoming a master of your strengths. As Raynor says, "Mediocre work fails to accomplish the essence of the Christian life: to serve others and to glorify God."[11]

The discipline of competency is true at the individual and at the organization level. In strategic management, we refer this as a firm's competitive advantage.[12] Resource-based theory informs us how to look inside a firm's unique resources and then to build a competitive advantage. There is great value in learning to develop a venture around a core strength.

Developing a competency takes discipline and endurance. Some argue that it takes roughly ten thousand hours of practice (about twenty hours a week for ten years) to become an excellent performer.[13] In *Outliers*, Malcolm Gladwell says that this rule is true across multiple skill areas like playing chess, computer programing, investing, and so forth.[14]

While genetics and environmental context matter, no one is born an expert. So, if you want your strengths to blossom into fruitfulness, then you need to take your talent and improve it through instruction, training, and practice, practice, practice!

The Discipline of Enjoying God in Your Talents

The Giver of gifts and talents wants you to know him better! Through his gifts to you, God is inviting you into a space for understanding more deeply how he thinks, aspects of his very nature, and how he constructed the universe. Our God-given talents and resources are not only outlets for impacting others, but they also represent highly useful channels for coming into a closer relationship with him.

Whether you're good at turning problems into new solutions or have an ability to bootstrap resources or systematize human behavior into computer code, God wants to connect with you. God gave you talents and resources to put into action, and he wants you to enjoy who you are through your talents and resources. Giftings are ways for better understanding yourself, your world, and most of all, your Creator.

Talents are like diamonds in the rough. With much cutting and crafting and polishing, a work of beauty is revealed. Although our talents are like those uncut diamonds, gains are still being made. Our talents are like windows into better understanding God and the beauty of his ways, and through your talents, you can come to love your work and also God!

The Parable of the Talents

"For it will be like a man going on a journey, who called his servants and entrusted to them his property. To one he gave five talents, to another two, to another one, to each according to his ability. Then he went away.

"He who had received the five talents went at once and traded with them, and he made five talents more. So also he who had the two talents made two talents more. But he who had received the one talent went and dug in the ground and hid his master's money.

"Now after a long time the master of those servants came and settled accounts with them. And he who had received the five talents came forward, bringing five talents more, saying, 'Master, you delivered to me five talents; here, I have made five talents more.'

"His master said to him, 'Well done, good and faithful servant. You have been faithful over a little; I will set you over much. Enter into the joy of your master.'

"And he also who had the two talents came forward, saying, 'Master, you delivered to me two talents; here, I have made two talents more.'

"His master said to him, 'Well done, good and faithful servant. You have been faithful over a little; I will set you over much. Enter into the joy of your master.'

"He also who had received the one talent came forward, saying, 'Master, I knew you to be a hard man, reaping where you did not sow, and gathering where you scattered no seed, so I was afraid, and I went and hid your talent in the ground. Here, you have what is yours.'

"But his master answered him, 'You wicked and slothful servant! You knew that I reap where I have not sown and gather where I scattered no seed? Then you ought to have invested my money with the bankers, and at my coming I should have received what was my own with interest. So take the talent from him and give it to him who has the ten talents. For to everyone who has will more be given, and he will have an abundance. But from the one who has not, even what he has will be taken away. And cast the worthless servant into the outer darkness. In that place there will be weeping and gnashing of teeth.'" (Matt. 25:14–30 ESV)

This fascinating parable from Jesus is set in the work context. With this parable, he sets a strong mandate for being prolific with our talents and resources in our work—and when we do this, we open up windows into discovering and enjoying God more deeply.

The "talent" Jesus refers to here was a unit of exchange of high financial worth equivalent to about fifteen to twenty years of common labor. The master in the parable gives out talents in the amount of five, two, and one to three different individuals. He then expects each servant to invest wisely based on their given *abilities*. He is planning to return, and in the meantime, they are to utilize their talent(s) to bring a return for his kingdom.

Two good servants invest wisely and double the value of what was entrusted to them. Likewise, we all have different talents and resources and in varying amounts, and we are also held responsible for making use of what we have been generously given. These talents and resources include those for conducting entrepreneurial trade. When we put our talents and resources into action, like the two good servants, we win the praise of the master. Then we are welcomed in as a dear friend to share in his joy and his goodness with special interactions.

Then there is the servant who buried the one talent he was given to invest, not even accruing interest on it. His errant view of God led to a wrong view of his talent and inactivity. Thus he faced eternal separation from God and all he desires to give us. Consider this abbreviated entrepreneurial paraphrase of the parable of the talents.

"This is Father God, and I'm getting ready to leave on a journey. Entrepreneur Emma, you're well gifted, so take these five bags worth about $1 million each, and invest them wisely with the skills you've been given. Entrepreneur Emily, in accordance with your giftings, here is $2 million. Go to work and invest it wisely with the skills you've been given. Entrepreneur Ella, here is $1 million. Go to work and invest it wisely in keeping with the skills you've been given."

After a long season away, Father God returned and wanted to settle his accounts. In response, Emma presented him with $10 million, and Emily had $4 million. Both Emma and Emily were highly praised and promised to be given much more when they get to heaven. "Come and share in my great joy!"

Then Ella came forward, handing Father God the original $1 million she was given. She offered her excuses for not making investments with her given skills. Upset with her, Father God said, "You didn't even gain any interest on this $1 million." He took the money from her and gave it to the one with $10 million, and then Ella was thrown into outer darkness.

The point of this parable is not just about being productive. It's about responding to God with the resources and talents he has given us. We have the option of being good and faithful stewards. When we do so, we get to know more of him and progressively come to share in the abundance of God's happiness. Nothing will ever be more satisfying!

If you desire to connect more with the God who is already in your workplace, then bring your giftedness to work. Your talents and resources are on loan to you from God. The more you use your gifts in the workplace, listen to offered feedback, and pursue training, the more new opportunities will emerge. The more you increase your competency with your giftings, the more likely you'll experience the God who is already at your work. Using your talents and resources in recognition of the Giver opens your soul to the winds of the Spirit.

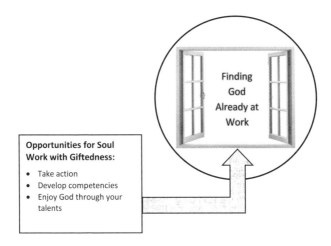

Chapter Model and Summary
Figure 5.1. Entrepreneurial Giftedness for Soul Work

Your Next Step

1. What are your strongest gifts and talents, and how are you increasing your expertise with it?

2. How are your gifts and talents opening your eyes to see more of God in your work?

6

Loving Your Workplace Neighbors

Gracious God, thank you for the great joy and privilege of being loved by you. Because you first lavished me with your love in Jesus, I have the privilege of responding to you in love. Out of your great abundance, enable me to generously love those with whom I interact at my work. Amen.

On his way to work at 6:30 a.m., Aaron swung by Starbucks for his usual latte. While standing in line, he met Elias, a twenty-six-year-old working in the gig economy. "What kind of work do you do?" asked Aaron.

"I do contract programming," Elias responded. "And last week I started a job for a company here in town, currently building out a voice and data network."

"How is it going so far?" Aaron asked, noting he seemed a little troubled.

"Good—until thirty minutes ago when someone walked by my table and knocked my laptop to the floor, busting the screen. This laptop is my livelihood. I don't know what I'm going to do."

How can Aaron be a "neighbor" to Elias, someone he has never met before? Besides, Aaron was also concerned about getting to his business to unlock the doors and start his employees on their day. Days like this, however, aren't exempt from what Jesus said about loving others.

Some two thousand years earlier, some religious leaders were wrangling with Jesus over details of the law but having little success. Then a top leader took one more crack at Jesus and asked, "Which commandment is the most important of all?" Jesus responded with the words recorded in Mark 12:29–31, "The Lord our God, the Lord is one. Love the Lord your God with all your heart and with all your soul and with all your mind and with all your strength. The second is this: Love your neighbor as yourself. There is no commandment greater than these." Another statement from Jesus that cut right to the core!

But what does it really mean to love the Creator of the universe, the redeemer, the righteous one who is sovereign over our lives with every ounce of our being, and to love our neighbor as ourselves?

I think that Jesus is saying that when the presence of God is in you, it is evidenced by your love for both God and neighbor.[1] "If you do these things you will live," he says, "not because they win for you eternal life, but because they demonstrate that eternal life is already yours, by grace alone through faith alone in Christ alone."[2]

For Aaron, he offered to let Elias, his new "neighbor," hang out at his business while he connected him to the local tech repair shop, which was set to open up at 9:00. This helped Elias and allowed Aaron to unlock his doors on time and get everyone started on their day.

Aaron will be the first to tell you he had second thoughts about helping Elias. Was Elias legitimate? Was this young man trustworthy? But the winds of the Spirit had been blowing through Aaron recently and he wanted to reach out more and love others. Maybe offering support to Elias was a next step for him. Shortly after 9:00, Aaron drove Elias to the tech support shop and by 1:30, he had a new screen installed and was back to work.

Is "Who Is My Neighbor?" the Right Question?

Following Jesus' declaration of the Greatest Commandment, a well-schooled religious lawyer asked the follow-up question recorded in Luke 10:29: "And who is my neighbor?" Luke says that this expert lawyer was seeking "to justify himself" and thereby minimize the breadth of his obedience to the law.[3]

Jesus, however, didn't let the message of the Greatest Commandment become restricted by narrow applications, contrived in-
terpretations, or additions to the law. Instead, Jesus challenged the
lawyer with the story about the good Samaritan in Luke 10:30–37.

> Jesus said: "A man was going down from Jerusalem to Jeri-
> cho, when he was attacked by robbers. They stripped him of
> his clothes, beat him and went away, leaving him half dead. A
> priest happened to be going down the same road, and when he
> saw the man, he passed by on the other side. So too, a Levite,
> when he came to the place and saw him, passed by on the other
> side. But a Samaritan, as he traveled, came where the man was;
> and when he saw him, he took pity on him. He went to him
> and bandaged his wounds, pouring on oil and wine. Then he
> put the man on his own donkey, brought him to an inn and
> took care of him. The next day he took out two denarii and gave
> them to the innkeeper. 'Look after him,' he said, 'and when I re-
> turn, I will reimburse you for any extra expense you may have.'

> "Which of these three do you think was a neighbor to the man
> who fell into the hands of robbers?"

> The expert in the law replied, "The one who had mercy on him."

> Jesus told him, "Go and do likewise."

Jesus flipped the expert lawyer's question on its head to ask,
"Who was the neighbor?" In other words, it's not principally about
identifying subgroups such as the people who live in my neighbor-
hood, in my department at work, in my part of town or even my
state. Being a neighbor is not about physical proximity or even
categories of family, best friends, colleagues, social status, race, or
gender. Being a neighbor means helping those who cannot or will
not give back. The victim in the parable was robbed, stripped of his
clothes, beaten, and lying on the side of the road, half dead. First,
a priest and then a Levite ignore him and quickly pass by on the
other side. The robbed man, who appeared dead on the side of the

road, was considered unclean for the priest and the Levite to touch. In fear of the Law, they turned a blind eye to him.

The good Samaritan in this parable might have been a merchant who traveled this road often. He was willing to give the innkeeper two denarii—two days' labor—in order to help the man recover from his injuries. It is this Samaritan, not the priest or the Levite, who was the true neighbor. He used his oil, wine, and money without any fanfare. Despite having a business to tend to, he made allowances for the injured man to receive genuine care.

In response to the lawyer's question, Jesus pointed him to be a "neighbor to the man who fell into the hands of the robbers" (Luke 10:36). Instead of asking who our neighbor is, we should ask what kind of neighbor *we are*. The call is to love even the unlovely. With one simple story, Jesus dissolved the contrived boundaries we create for limiting our neighborliness.

On Seeing God

How do we get to a point of genuinely loving God and our neighbors? First John 4:7–21 offers complementary insights. Loving God and neighbor actually opens our spiritual windows. Verse 12 is particularly compelling: "No one has ever seen God; but if we love one another, God lives in us and his love is made complete in us."

Loving God with everything we have and our neighbors as ourselves is impossible on our own. If we are to offer an all-out love for God and neighbors, then we must first receive the love God offers us. Love starts with God. When we start absorbing his perfect and unconditional love, we can then respond to God and others with love. "We love because he first loved us" (1 John 4:19). With his permeating love, God changes us to love him and our neighbors. What a foundational truth on which to anchor our journey forward. With this kind of soul work, we can increasingly respond in love to our God and neighbors.

When we respond to his love by loving others, thinking here specifically of those in our workplace, God's love can rise to new heights within us! While we do not get to see God's face this side of heaven, we can experience his ever-increasing presence deeper within. As our souls pant for God (Ps. 42:1), our love-tank begins to fill with God's love. We can then love others without any concern for reputation, and God's presence takes up residence inside us! By extending ourselves to love others, imperfect though it may be, God's love swells within us and becomes more refined.

This perspective then opens up our workplaces as amazing frontiers for us to refine the kind of "neighbor" we are becoming. If you want to see more of God, then it is worth an all-out effort to probe new ways of loving others in your work.

Loving Others as Opportunities for Soul Work

I have squandered more than my share of opportunities to love others at work. There was the competitor who compromised the job so that he could obtain the winning bid, but I let this incident become a wall to any further dealings with him. There was the employee who was uncooperative when a job called for a joint effort, but I let his subsequent distance became a barrier between us. Then there was the time a contractor's truck and many tools were stolen, but I did nothing to help him get back on the job. Other times, I helped a person in the workplace, but only with the "silent" motivation of building up my own reputation. And on I could go.

My failure to love these folks without any self-serving motives truncated any opportunity for soul work. It left my love-bucket empty. If you're already receiving at least some of Jesus' love and you long for more, then consider your workplace opportunities for pursuing conversation, forgiveness, compassion, and generosity. Open your window so the winds of the Holy Spirit can more readily come on you.

Engage in Conversation

Once I learn that someone has a significantly different worldview, political persuasion, or different ethical practices, I tend to shy away from further conversation. But such individuals are still my neighbors. I do well to learn from people like Daryl Davis.

Daryl, a Black musician, was playing in a club one evening when a Ku Klux Klan member struck up a conversation with him. It was Daryl's first conversation with a Klansman, and it was the Klansman's first conversation with a Black person. As recorded in the documentary *Accidental Courtesy*,[4] Daryl decided to seize the opportunity to try and become a friend of the Klansman. He hoped that their interaction and friendship would lead him to abandon the KKK's harmful ideology. Over time, Daryl initiated more conversations, and they went on outings together, like a trip to Lowe's, to give them excuses to relate.

Although as their friendship grew, so did this Klansman's rank within KKK, and he eventually became their national leader. "But Daryl was always there for him; never judged him, never turned to rhetoric in telling him he was wrong. Daryl just loved him the way we who know Christ calls us to love one another, to love as he has loved us."[5] After a long-developed friendship, the Klansman saw enough problems with the Klan's ideology to make the decision to leave. To date, Daryl has befriended a multitude of Klansmen, resulting in more than two hundred of them leaving the Klan.

If the Holy Spirit is nudging you to practice the discipline of conversation, here are the key points that Daryl offers:

- Talk with the other person. We spend far too much time talking at, about, and past other people. When two enemies are talking, they are not fighting.

- Listen and understand the way they think instead of beating up on them.

- Thoroughly inform yourself of the other perspective.

- Many people struggle with their own ideology. Talking about it with someone else usually lets them confront the challenges of their own views.

- When you invest in relationships, differences between us matter less and less.[6]

How often do you engage your neighbor in good conversation, even when their views differ widely? From the list above, what do you need most to work on?

Forgiveness

If you reach out and offer love to your neighbors at work (or anywhere), some of them will most likely be offended. When this happens, you need to be ready to apologize or perhaps forgive. If you don't, then this could become a barrier between you and the other person, and between you and God. As Paul writes, "Bear with each other and forgive one another if any of you has a grievance against someone. Forgive as the Lord forgave you" (Col. 3:13). And "be kind and compassionate to one another, forgiving each other, just as in Christ God forgave you" (Eph. 4:32).

We are all much too flawed to be involved in meaningful relationships without needing the means of forgiveness available to us. I can reach out to a coworker, but if I say something that's offensive to them, I get pushback. Although I was on my way to first base with a new relationship, I learn that they now talk negatively of me to others. It's like lending an item to a colleague only to have it damaged or even not returned.

If we're going to become a good neighbor to others, then we need Jesus and his model of forgiveness in a big way. Write down the offenses and wounds that come your way and then forgive. Without forgiveness, walls will be erected and you will become a lousy neighbor.

But forgiveness is so much easier to discussion than accomplish. Just acknowledging the reality of the hurt can be an issue, and then there's the actual forgiveness process. Often, if I've forgiven this person, additional offenses follow. Then it feels like the wounding sticks to me like Velcro or salt is put on old wounds.

Getting to the place of forgiveness never seems to be easy. When I did get to a place of forgiveness, the offense still hovered over me. Then through a season of learning including multiple offenses along with my own trials and errors, a three-step approach began to emerge. Step A is coming to acknowledge the pain of the offense. Without fully owning the pain of the offense personally, I found my journey to forgiveness truncated. Only after this is accomplished can we meaningfully move into Step B and forgiveness. Step C then extends into our fuller journey with God. Below are three steps facilitating this process.

A. *Acknowledging the pain and owning it: Specify three or more words that describe your hurt, such as abandoned, angry, betrayed, rejected, etc. Then note the pain level from 1–10, with 10 being the highest intensity of pain. Make sure to take the necessary time (minutes, hours, or even days) to fully own this pain before moving on to Step B. If you do not articulate and own the offense and your specific pain, then you have not yet set the stage for Step B and forgiveness.*

I feel hurt by *[name the person]* _____

for *[identify the offense]* _____

_____

This caused me to feel _____ [1–10], _____ [1–10],

and _____ [1–10].

B. *Forgiving:*

Based on the blood of Jesus and the forgiveness he offers to me, I choose to forgive *[name the person]*, and I willingly suffer and accept the emotional pain and consequences that this offense has caused me. Now I pray, help me not to waste this pain. I accept the death that I need to die. I accept this opportunity to experience fellowship with Jesus in his suffering. I exchange the suffering of this offense for another wound—that of the crucified Lord Jesus. With this wounding, I gain further understanding of your suffering; I lean into you. Holy Spirit, by your power, take this wounding and turn it into a channel to bond with Jesus and the Father more deeply. I ask you, take back the ground I gave to the enemy through my carrying of this offense and for resisting the carrying of this cross that you have asked me to bear. I yield this ground to your control. I trust you to be true and just.

C. Deepening your journey forward:

Thank you, Father, for this trial and the good that you are working to bring from it. By the power of Jesus' blood, I can lay down this burden. With the help of the Holy Spirit, I have forgiven! The work of forgiveness is now being accomplished in my soul. The deepest desire of my heart is to be with you. Bring your resurrection within me! Use this wound to draw me in, to lift more of the veil from my eyes so that I might know more of your glory.

I keep the above paragraphs on an electronic file. Then when an offense comes, I pull out this skeletal process and start to revamp the paragraphs to fit the current offense I'm experiencing. These paragraphs continue to evolve as my wounding and my understanding of God moves forward. Consider tailoring these paragraphs to make them your own.

Step A is critical for starting the forgiveness process. If I don't first allow myself the freedom to truly own the hurts of the offense, then the following two steps are largely frivolous. I must fully acknowledge the offense and the pain. Otherwise, the forgiveness process becomes ineffective, and the walls fail to come down.

Forgiving our offenders based on the work Jesus did on the cross is an amazing gift. His forgiveness of my sins allows me to forgive others and then to receive more of his love. As noted above, forgiving others is a part of receiving Jesus' forgiveness. Furthermore, Jesus says in Matthew 6:14, "For if you forgive others their trespasses, your heavenly Father will also forgive you."

If the parties to an offense can come together and face the committed wrongs with forgiveness, then there can be reconciliation. But discussions over an offense are not always possible. If we're hurt by the way a superior dealt with a situation, or the way someone walked off the job, or the way a customer bad-mouthed our product, one-on-one reconciliation may not be possible. We still, however, have the option and even obligation to forgive. Forgiving frees us from the anger within and liberates our heart to draw near to God. It also opens the door for future communication with the offender, should the opportunity arise.

Forgiveness is an incredible means for advancing our relationship with God. When we fail to forgive others, not only is that relationship likely minimized or even lost, but our relationship with God is damaged and reaching out to others in love is hindered. In Luke 6:37, Jesus says, "Forgive, and you will be forgiven." Forgiving others serves as evidence of God living in us, and it opens our personal doors for more of him and others!

Compassion

The parable of the good Samaritan models compassion toward a badly injured man. When someone has a need, it's rarely convenient for us and always seems to be more complicated than we'd like. It takes a heart that is being changed by God to cut through the difficulties of any situation. Ask God to grow your compassion, and then allow it to guide your decision-making. Consider these practices to gain more compassion for others in the workplace.

- Take time to understand the concerns and stressors of your colleagues. Let your heart move with compassion toward them (Matt. 14:14–16).

- Bless others by communicating how much you appreciate their work.

- If someone is underappreciated or even exploited, become an advocate for that person.

Generosity

Out of compassion is likely to come generosity. The good Samaritan was successful enough to be able to pay for the medical needs and lodging for an injured stranger. He even put his business on hold while he spent money and time to care for that stranger.

What an encouragement from someone who probably had significant demands on his time. As in this parable, Jesus shows us that loving others takes effort and resources, and it always seems to come at an inconvenient time. Here are some ways to practice generosity in your workplace:

- Look for opportunities to take someone to lunch.

- Hold your possessions loosely so you can lend them to others.

- Offer to jump in on a current problem someone may be grappling with.

A generous spirit is a great tool in being the kind of neighbor who honors Jesus.

Parable of the Good Samaritan: Round 2

Let's finish this chapter with another look at the parable of the good Samaritan as it is the perfect example of how we can love our "neighbors" in the workplace.

I find it constructive to note the contrast between the "expert in the law" and the Samaritan in the parable, especially as the picture is quite vivid. Consider the differences below between the two players in this story.

	The Lawyer	The Good Samaritan
Concern	Worried if his neighborliness fit within his categories of who his neighbors were	Free to meet an obvious need
Response time	Ignored the immediate need because it did not fit into his schedule	Responded to the immediate need
Race	Racial boundaries	No racial boundaries
Thought life	Focused on his own purity over the other's need	Focused on others and cared about what was needed
Moral behavior	Out of self-righteousness, responded without love	Out of love, responded rightly to the need
Motivation	Concerned with meeting the letter of the law	Open to opportunities to love others

The question now becomes how we can get to the point of loving our neighbors in need. Addressing this challenge involves getting beyond just trying to do the right thing according to the law. As Dallas Willard has noted, "[Jesus] knew that we cannot keep the law by trying to keep the law. To succeed in *keeping* the law one must aim at something other and something more."[7] So, what is to be our target?

The aim is to be transformed from the inside out by what—or rather who—is behind the law. When we are adopted into God's family by the work of Jesus, his redeeming blood now flows through our veins. The love of Jesus can now flow through us to others.

Being compelled by the love of God, we can now genuinely and spontaneously respond with compassion to those on our pathways.

Concern for our reputation with customers, worry over the agenda of our meeting, possible financial costs, or fear of injury or disease—these should all fall behind the more immediate needs of our coworkers. The more we open ourselves up to God first loving us, the more we will want to respond with compassion when needs emerge in front of us on our various roads to Jericho. We become compelled to meet the needs of those around us in response to the lavish love God has given us.

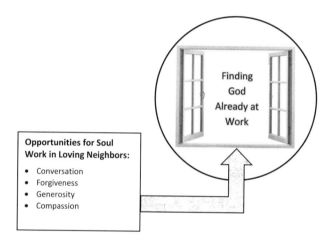

Opportunities for Soul Work in Loving Neighbors:

- Conversation
- Forgiveness
- Generosity
- Compassion

Finding God Already at Work

Chapter Model and Summary
Figure 6.1. Entrepreneurial Love for Soul Work

Loving our neighbor as ourselves is an impossible mission. Fortunately, God loved us first and put his seeds of love and life in us. Consequently, we can grow in becoming the kind of neighbors at work who feed the souls of others along with our own. God is already at your work in the individuals he has put in your pathway. When you reach out to those in need, you further open your own window to soul work within.

Would you like to connect more with the God who is already in the needs of people in your workplace? Then develop your conversation skills. Become vigilant in dealing with your own heart wounds by drawing on the available gift of forgiveness we have available in Jesus. Become a student of compassion and generosity. While exercising these disciplines doesn't guarantee God's presence, with right motivates, they can open our windows to allow the winds of the Holy Spirit to blow within.

Your Next Step

1. Loving your neighbor with the right motives is only possible if you're first open to letting God rain his love on you. What are your needs? Where are you aware of your own need for the Holy Spirit to make his love more real in you to others?

2. Of the four work disciplines of engaging conversation, forgiveness, generosity, and compassion, which one is your biggest barrier to loving your neighbors?

7

COMPASSIONATE JUSTICE
FOR SOUL WORK

Our Father, "Your kingdom come, your will be done, on earth as it is in heaven" (Matt. 6:10). Grant us, Lord, your vision for the world we live in. Free people to engage in good work and receive fair compensation. Bring about a world where all races and cultures live in harmony with mutual respect; where peace is built with justice and justice is guided by love. Give us the inspiration and courage to build it, through Jesus Christ our Lord. Amen.

Scenario #1. "Lowell, do you have time to help Harry with a bathroom cabinet?" asked Marvin, a brother with whom I worshiped. "He's a neighbor of yours and needs a modification to accommodate his new wheelchair. He lives by himself and is in his eighties with little money."

"Yes," I responded. "I'll go over there and see if I can make Harry's bathroom functional."

A week later, after a half-day of work, Harry's bathroom was now wheelchair functional.

But under the surface, my attitude was poor. I was open to helping the "Harrys" of my world with my work skills. At this point, however, I knew little about the joy in giving. I was focused on bigger jobs and building my business. Consequently, this "giving" accomplished no soul work in me.

Thirty-five years later, I'm still embarrassed about my bad attitude with helping the Harrys of my world. More importantly, by passing on such opportunities, I squandered countless opportunities for soul work. I missed the blessing of giving to others.

Scenario #2. "Hey Lowell," said Miles when he stopped by. "It looks like you're making some good progress on this construction project."

"Yes," I said. "About three more days, and I should have this job wrapped up, weather permitting."

Then Miles said, "By the way, I just heard the city has some low-income grants for renovating homes in our town. Do you know anything about these projects?"

"Yes, I won a bid for one of their projects about three months ago. It was a reasonable job, and I found the city personnel good to work with. Would you like to get connected so you could bid on these projects?"

In short, with my help, Miles became qualified for bidding on future contracts.

For each round of bidding, each contractor could win no more than one bid. When the next round of contracts came in six weeks later, Miles put in his bids. Unfortunately, he didn't win any of the bids because the notoriously low bidder on these projects, R&S Construction,[1] put in bids under multiple names. R&S was a family business owned and operated by a father and two sons. The father and both sons each submitted their own individual bids under separate names, even though all the work would be done as one unit. Consequently, they beat Miles on winning any bids.

Although this family may have technically followed the right procedure to win these bids, they were skirting the spirit of the law. Miles felt he had been cheated, so I went with him to the city to issue a complaint, but the issue couldn't be remedied.

However, coming alongside Miles spoke volumes to him. R&S's manipulation of the contractual guidelines wasn't right, but this injustice did become a bridge in my relationship with Miles.

Aligning Workplace Justice

Our world gets ugly far too often, but we know that God is just and that justice is a pillar of his character. Psalm 89:14 says, "Righteousness and justice are the foundation of your throne; love and faithfulness go before you." God's justice was also evident in Jesus' earthly life. He repeatedly looked with heartfelt compassion on the poor, the children, and the sick. Even those socially distanced by leprosy and various diseases were touched by him.

Most of us know that helping the poor and sharing with those less fortunate is the right thing to do. But sometimes it's not until we have personally experienced God's grace that we find ourselves increasingly desirous of extending that same compassion and justice to others.

Questions invariably emerge about where to jump in and get involved in a meaningful way. Where and how can we help make a difference? Attempts to address social ills invariably falls short. Social problems tend to be complex and challenging to address, and meaningful contributions can be illusive.

The story of Ruth in the Bible provides us with a refreshing example. Being widowed and an immigrant with the thinnest of resources, she is rescued by Boaz, the relative of her mother-in-law, Naomi. Tom Nelson writes, "Boaz's affirmation of Ruth's human dignity, provision of physical safety, and willingness to offer her access to productive work are instructive for us today."[2] With her marriage to Boaz, Ruth later becomes a mother and eventually the great-grandmother of King David and therefore in the ancestral line to Jesus.

Although we all want to contribute to poverty and justice issues as we see with Ruth, the related challenges often overwhelm us. Thankfully, countless organizations are passionate about meeting the human, economic, and spiritual needs of those who are at critical points of need. Unfortunately, the gifts and services offered by such organizations address only the immediate needs. Giving someone struggling with an addiction shelter and clothing may help for a while, but we need to move such a person to a more flourishing life, which can be most challenging.

As potential contributors, we are often asked to give in ways that don't mesh with our own strengths and gifts. There are countless opportunities to give money to organizations that are passionate about defined human, economic, or spiritual needs. However, just giving of resources does little to develop within us a heart of compassion for the needy and for justice. The lack of a match on both sides of this coin is a recipe for failure. With a lack of match, the human, economic, and spiritual needs are rarely met. And the "givers" come away from a mismatch feeling unmoved or even disenchanted.

Given the many human needs surrounding us, perhaps you've found yourself thinking that there has to be a more constructive path forward. How do you meaningfully get involved with a situation and extend some compassion? We want to see more of God, but we often don't know how to get started. This chapter is about uncovering entry points where you can engage with social needs and do so in a way that facilitates soul work.

Honoring the Dignity of Work

If you're willing to engage in compassionate justice, then consider your roots—your deep roots. Genesis 1:27 tells us that "God created mankind in his own image." As to the meaning of "image," Tim Keller says it expresses "the idea of being a work of art or of great craftsmanship. Human beings are not accidents, but creations."[3] All of us resemble aspects of God's image. What a profound statement of our origins.

From this premise, Keller writes, "Every human life is sacred and every human being has dignity."[4] It thrills me when I see someone use a welder to craft pieces of steel into a new tool, or when someone uses their financial skills to resolve a problem or gain insight into business, marriage, or the spiritual condition. I believe it thrills God as well. We are all God's developing work of art!

Dignity in our work emerges when we engage both body and mind. The ability to analyze, interpret, and respond in our work brings dignity.[5] Our work also enables us to earn a wage and thus engage in economic exchanges. The obtainment of economic resources enables us to provide for the necessities of life and build toward acceptable values.

Now consider the flip side of not working. Research by the Pew Research Center found that nearly 38 percent of people who were unemployed for six months or longer reported a loss of self-respect.[6] To be without work is to be unable to provide for one's family and oneself, to be cut off from individual accomplishments and from socialization, and to be restricted in one's personal development.

Individual dignity emerges from work. And even more so when we can pursue work where our personal strengths are allowed to grow and contribute to a larger purpose as a part of a team. Since work is almost always accomplished in teams, it dovetails with our need for human socializing. It is also dignifying for us to be able to engage our minds with problem solving, to work in teams, and to contribute to the good of others. Work is good!

The dignity of work is central to addressing social needs and justice issues. Dignity is foundational to those of us who seek to constructively contribute to injustices and to those who find themselves in impoverished and disadvantaged situations. When we engage dignity, human flourishing abounds.

In their influential book *When Helping Hurts*, Steve Corbett and Brian Fikkert build the case for discerning whether the situation calls for relief, rehabilitation, or development.[7] The relief stage is relevant to a crisis when a hurricane displaces people or when someone is the victim of a robbery or becomes ill. The second stage of rehabilitation involves coming alongside others to help provide encouragement, instruction, and resources to enable them to rebuild their lives. Examples include helping clean up a home after a flood or provide the needed training to recover from an unexpected job loss. The final stage of development is about the ongoing process of coming alongside people as they make the necessary adjustments to better fulfill their calling. The goal is to move both the "helpers" and the "helped" to be "in right relationship with God, self, others, and the rest of creation."[8] In this framework, entrepreneurial opportunities may lie in the areas of rehabilitation but particularly in the development stage.

Entrepreneurial Justice

Social entrepreneurship involves the process of building sustainable business models around social issues. A social entrepreneur is one who explores business opportunities that have a positive impact on their community and larger society. The real strength of social entrepreneurship is the ability to take strategic action to address a social need with an economic model. When a viable business model is implemented, meeting the social need then becomes scalable and sustainable.

For example, the lack of safe drinking water across many areas of the globe claims lives each year. As a result, multiple charities have emerged with pockets full of donations to drill new wells in needy communities. Realizing that the water crisis won't be solved with the charity model, Water4 (Water4.org) discovered that significant inroads could be made by empowering people to meet their own needs with the assistance of a business model and by creating local jobs.

Water4 set out to design a state-of-the-art manual drilling rig to facilitate percussion drilling. Franchisees located in the country and community of need can scale quickly and efficiently with local entrepreneurs and workers at a fraction of the cost of traditionally drilled boreholes. With the local presence and the help of the business model, the Water4 model facilitates accountability and repair alternatives. New local companies now repair and fix problems that arise.

Water4 was started by Richard and Terri Greenly. They have long been co-owners of Pumps of Oklahoma, a wholesaler distributor and manufacturer of water well drilling, pumping and water treatment equipment. In 2005, Richard had the opportunity to help bring clean drinking water to the people of a remote community in

China. From his professional experience and his involvement with the world water crisis, he chose to become a part of the solution by employing his entrepreneurial skills and giftings to create Water4.

Business, when done right, has an amazing capacity to contribute to the global good. Water4 is an example of how entrepreneurship is emerging as a way of compassionately extending justice. And like Richard and Terri with Water4, there are many opportunities for impact when people extend their developed entrepreneurial skills and resources. Many of our social ills can be greatly aided by the application of entrepreneurial endeavors done right. Using our skills and capabilities to involve ourselves with a justice issue adds to our own dignity and enables us to reflect our God to others.

Pursuing Compassionate Justice

The rock-solid foundation for extending compassionate justice builds first from the reality that God owns everything. "To the LORD your God belong the heavens, even the highest heavens, the earth and everything in it" (Deut. 12:14). And given that "we brought nothing into the world, and we can take nothing out of it" (1 Tim. 6:7), we have incredible opportunities to use what he has provided to extend his justice.

Do you desire to extend justice? Consider then how you can extend your entrepreneurial capabilities into the corners of injustice in your world. What can you do to breathe new life into an injustice in your work domain? Below I probe several areas to stir your thinking. Furthermore, extending compassionate justice has the potential to change your heart. Pursuing justice opens the personal windows of our heart so the winds of the Holy Spirit can reach in.

Recognize God's Ownership

Find something to give to others every day to remind yourself that everything you have is the Lord's to begin with. Even though we are co-creators, everything we use in our creation processes comes from him. Given that the earth and everything in it belongs to the Lord, how can you use the resources currently on loan to help you lean into the door of compassionate justice? Consider the following ideas:

- Take the stranger, the shunned, the "thirsty," the marginalized for coffee or even a meal. Allow yourself to listen to them—really listen. If you can do that, then you will learn firsthand about the injustices around you.

- Offer mentoring to those who have few or no opportunities for learning from experienced individuals like yourself.

- Help an underprivileged individual get into an appropriate training workshop to help them grow in an area of expertise they're interested in.

- Provide consulting or seed capital to an underprivileged individual who desires to start a business.

See the Injustices around You

While there are notable large-scale problems that require action, be careful not to miss the injustices around you. Consider the following who may need your help:

- An employee or colleague who is buried in the court system and whose work performance has dropped.

- Someone who received an unfair performance review because of jealousy or stereotype.

- An employee without transportation because their car was stolen or requires expensive repairs.

- A person of color who suffers microaggressions in the workplace and whose authority is undermined by coworkers.

- An entrepreneur who is called bossy or overbearing because of her gender.

- An employee who receives unwanted comments or physical touch from coworkers.

Sometimes people subjected to injustice need a listening ear or emotional support and reminders of their individual worth. Other times, they may need help getting to the right lawyer or other expertise outside their normal contacts.

Start a Social Venture

Further to our discussion on Jesus' parable, here's a follow-on from Tim Keller: "Imagine a sequel to the Good Samaritan parable. The months go by and every time the Good Samaritan makes his trip from Jerusalem to Jericho, he finds another man in the road, beaten and robbed. Finally the Samaritan says, 'How do we stop the violence?'"[9]

Does this idea move you? Could you do something with your entrepreneurial skills and experience to reflect this righteous Samaritan? Consider these questions:

- What social problems do you keep seeing in your workplace pathway around which you or someone else could build a business model?

- Is there a market void with a disadvantaged people group that your business could extend into? Human, social, and natural capital along with financial capital can be mobilized for the good of all.[10]

As modeled in Figure 7.1, when we extend ourselves into areas of compassionate justice, significant opportunities for soul repair and uniting with Jesus become possible.

The Parable of the Lost Sheep

Now the tax collectors and sinners were all gathering around to hear Jesus. But the Pharisees and the teachers of the law muttered, "This man welcomes sinners and eats with them."

Then Jesus told them this parable: "Suppose one of you has a hundred sheep and loses one of them. Doesn't he leave the ninety-nine in the open country and go after the lost sheep until he finds it? And when he finds it, he joyfully puts it on his shoulders and goes home. Then he calls his friends and neighbors together and says, 'Rejoice with me; I have found my lost sheep.' I tell you that in the same way there will be more rejoicing in heaven over one sinner who repents than over ninety-nine righteous persons who do not need to repent."

(Luke 15:1–7)

This parable has significant implications for our pursuit of compassionate justice in our interactions with individuals connected to our workplace. I now offer an extended paraphrase of this powerful parable through an entrepreneurial lens.

"Kevin, are you okay?" asked Lucas the owner of this quality cabinet business with a hundred employees. "You seem distracted and withdrawn."

"Not really," Kevin replied. "But I'll get through it. It's something I don't want to talk about right now." Kevin is the IT guy for the business who has kept their computer network singing beautifully. Some of the other ninety-nine employees also express concern for Kevin.

Four days later, he doesn't show up for work. On the second day of being a no-show, Lucas starts phoning him, but Kevin doesn't answer. Then Lucas goes by his home. After three trips, still no sign of Kevin. Then he remembers Kevin saying how much he enjoyed a national park about three hundred miles away. The next morning, Lucas gets into his pickup and drives to the park. During the second day of searching the vast area, Lucas finally found him. He looked in bad shape as if in a dark hole emotionally.

"Kevin!" called Lucas. "We've been worried about you! We've missed you! What's going on?"

After getting over the shock of Lucas finding him, Kevin finally told him, "I lost my total net worth of $85,000 from a real estate deal gone bad. I've lost everything." Kevin was trying to rise above his humble upbringing. He is devastated and contemplating suicide.

After talking with him for several hours, Lucas then packed him up in his truck and took him back to his home. The next day, he arranges for Kevin to receive the psychological and legal help he needs and covers all the expenses. Although he still had a long way to go, Kevin was able to confront some deep flaws and call on Jesus. Kevin was now ready to return to work.

When he returns, Lucas is ecstatic to see Kevin's changed demeanor. He's so excited that he announces to the company, "Come rejoice with me with a Friday afternoon celebration! Kevin is back!"

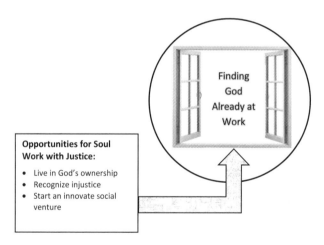

Chapter Model and Summary
Figure 7.1. Compassionate Justice for Soul Work

Given the challenging road of becoming proactive with the injustices around us, it's critical to have two foundation stones in place. The first is understanding that God's ownership is comprehensive. He owns the earth and everything in it. What we have is on loan from him, so it becomes a privilege to extend those resources to others to make the world a little more just. The second foundation stone is knowing the grace given to us by Jesus' sacrificial life for our personal wrongs. With these foundation stones in place, it becomes a privilege to be an active proponent of justice. In the words of Acts 20:35, "It is more blessed to give than to receive." When we give without a desire to be noticed, without ulterior motivates, the window opens for significant soul work.

Consider enriching your soul by finding at least one way to become proactive for compassionate justice in your work. Consciously look for an injustice with which you can closely connect. Perhaps even consider starting a social venture that wraps a business model around a social need. Actively pursue compassionate justice and be blessed Consider these powerful words from Isaiah 58:5–7 (NLT):

> "No, this is the kind of fasting I want: Free those who are wrongly imprisoned; lighten the burden of those who work for you. Let the oppressed go free, and remove the chains that bind people. Share your food with the hungry, and give shelter to the homeless. Give clothes to those who need them, and do not hide from relatives who need your help."

Your Next Step

1. Of the three practices of living in God's ownership, an injustice before your eyes, or starting an entrepreneurial venture, is the Holy Spirit nudging you toward one?

2. From your previous efforts with injustices, was there a time or event when you felt that significant soul work was accomplished? Why?

8

THE "VALLEY OF DEATH" FOR SOUL WORK

O God, I am surrounded by much greed, stealing, deceptions, and pain. I sometimes wonder where your presence is. But your Spirit remains strong around me. Empower me to put my eyes on you when troubles in my workplace arise. Oh God, strengthen me in you as I walk through these dark valleys. Only because of my Jesus-grounded faith can I consider it a privilege to participate in sufferings, thus accomplishing significant soul work. Amen.

"Three years ago, I launched BridgeVR, offering a virtual reality concept for the physical therapy sector," said Leslie. With a semi-successful exit of a software venture with application into the dental space and then three years as VP of product development for a medical device company, Leslie already has more entrepreneurial experience at the age of thirty-six than most people achieve in a lifetime.

Leslie further told me, "With BridgeVR, I have now invested all my money from my first venture, I have two equity investors on board with their investments, and now my line of credit of $100,000 is maxed out. I have two physical therapy offices successfully utilizing my BridgeVR platform, but I have yet to get the larger physical therapy operations with multiple centers on board. My two equity investors are getting nervous and threatening to pull the plug, even though they earlier promised funding for another year."

She then expressed that this past year had been tougher than nails. "I can still project optimism to my investors, employees, and potential clients—but inside, my nerves are tight as a drum. Privately, I find myself wondering if this venture will survive the 'valley of death.'"

"Two months ago, I was feeling things couldn't get any worse, but then my lead video graphics programmer quit. What really hurt was another VR business hired him away by leveling a false accusation against me, and now BridgeVR's development of further physical therapy applications is on hold. Then the day after his resignation, my very supportive father was rushed to the emergency room with heart failure."

These challenges left Leslie with several deeper questions:

- Does God even care about this venture? I've prayed and committed it to him, but I'm not hearing anything from God right now.

- When it rains, it pours. Is this wave of problems all about Satan trying to bring me down?

- Are my problems God's punishment for my earlier wrongs?

- Is there any soul work emerging from this troubling season?

Spiritual Pain in the Workplace

Nothing raises more questions and is more challenging to understand than pain and hard times. Troubles and hardships are common in the workplace as well as personal lives, although the discussion rarely gets beyond whether those involved are "living right."

How do we make sense of the halting work on a major innovation project due to a lawsuit? Maybe a $30,000 piece of equipment is ruined by falling off the back of a truck. Or some animosity between coworkers is strangling a project. After a tough day like Leslie's, maybe you find yourself asking, "Does God even care about my work?"

Experiencing workplace challenges and pain are rarely seen as anything having to do with our relationship with our God. When the sacred/secular divide (which we discussed in chapter 1) is a part of our mindset, then workplace trials are seldom seen through a spiritual lens. We can readily give "spiritual" attention to challenges with ministry activities, but we rarely give such attention to when things don't go right in the workplace.

With a sacred/secular divide perspective, we likely see suffering in the workplace as having limited spiritual relevance. Problems are the cost of doing business. The "legitimate" suffering comes from sharing the gospel or some other explicit spiritual activity.

But challenges and hardships are common to the entire human race, including those who work—which is pretty much everybody. Genesis 3:17 says, "Cursed is the ground because of you; through painful toil you will eat food from it all the days of your life." Ever since the fall of Adam and Eve, our work is by the sweat of our brows. The evil one got his way with Adam and Eve, and this condition won't change this side of heaven.

Dealing with fraud, conflict, and broken stuff is part of living in a world with both light and dark present. This also becomes a spiritual issue for those of us seeking God. God is everywhere, including the hardships and pains of our work. He is big enough to sometimes "allow what he hates to accomplish what he loves."[1]

But we often get tangled with hardships issues because the "why" question is lurking. Jesus addressed this when asked about a man born blind and whether this happened because of the sin of the blind man or his parents. In John 9:3, Jesus responded, "Neither. . . . This happened so that the works of God might be displayed in him." What a statement!

Jesus also left an example of suffering for us. Additionally, the Scriptures are clear about the positive impact trials and suffering have on our growth. For example, 1 Peter 1:7 says, "These have come so that the proven genuineness of your faith—of greater worth than gold, which perishes even though refined by fire—may result in praise, glory and honor when Jesus Christ is revealed." There is a prize for endearing perseverance! Our faith will come to be worth more than pure gold, which takes us into the territory of unspeakable joy! Faith in our suffering will stand as evidence in our victories and will be displayed during our ultimate homecoming in heaven.

A central point here is that the curse is a reality for everyone; its impact is just as true for those in full-time ministry as it is for Jesus-following entrepreneurs. It is true for all. In Matthew 5:45, Jesus says, "He causes his sun to rise on the evil and the good, and sends rain on the righteous and the unrighteous."

Suffering in the workplace is something God allows. Furthermore, hardships and trials are major tools God uses to unite us with him, and they have great potential to stimulate growth and intimacy with our Savior.

C. S. Lewis famously said, "God whispers to us in our pleasures, speaks in our conscience, but shouts in our pain."[2] When things go according to plan, we tend to be satisfied and do little to draw closer to God. But when workplace hardships come our way, they can readily serve to open wider our channels with God.

Job's Story

Job's story is so fascinating and powerful because of the depth of his pain. Most importantly, it ultimately served to connect himself with God much more closely.[3]

As a successful rancher, businessman, father, and husband, the demise of Job's world around him started with his work context as recorded for us in Job 1:13–19. First, the Sabeans made off with his oxen and donkeys and servants. This was followed by fire coming down and destroying his sheep and servants. Then the Chaldeans stole all his camels and killed even more servants. Finally, a great wind took down the house where his children were, killing all inside.

Later, Job takes his complaints before the Lord. In 24:2, he says, "There are those who move boundary stones; they pasture flocks they have stolen." In other words, there are ranchers laying claim to other people's land (most likely, Job's) to graze their herds. And there are those who steal other ranchers' livestock, as Job experienced (see Job 1:13–19 as referenced above).

Job never gives up on God. He also speaks candidly of what's on his mind from the depth of his pain. He finds God to be totally worthy of his faith, even when he is unrelenting and hard. God is still the creator and sustainer of life and worthy of all our loyalties, honor, and love. God longs for us to connect with him, and pain has a way of opening the channels. With our intense suffering, our emotions are laid bare, and we often find our Lord coming near.

But there is another side. When competitors want to destroy your business or a storm wipes out your buildings or a customer proves ruthless, this is a reminder of how Satan inflicts his darkness on us, doing his best to derail us and cause us to doubt God. But our God is greater, and God extends to us his overwhelming grace and power to move closer to him.

In response to a natural disaster, it's common to say, "My business is ruined. I don't know if I'll be able to build back. How can a loving God cause such widespread and indiscriminate destruction?"

But in response to such devastation, there are also gains to be had and we can say, "It took weeks of blood, sweat, and tears to clean up the wreckage. For weeks I cried out to God 'Why?' and 'Why my business?' But after fifteen months of rebuilding, I have a very different perspective. This may have been the best thing to ever happen to my business. It gave me the opportunity to rebuild with a reconfigured business model to fit the changing marketplace. More importantly, I'm a changed person on the inside, and I learned a deeper dependence on God. I'm now much closer to God."

These two contrasting responses can be called the "suffering paradox." By the power of the Spirit, we have the opportunity take a devastating event and let God work his mighty ways.

Don't miss the concluding interactions between God and Job. God renders no condemnation of Job, but he also doesn't apologize or given any reasons for the trials Job had to endure, nor does he praise Job for standing strong as God claimed in the first chapter. In fact, God turns the table and begins his interrogation of Job, asking over seventy unanswerable questions.[4]

About the conclusion of the book of Job, Philip Yancey makes the following observation:

> Sidestepping thirty-five chapters' worth of debates on the problem of pain, he [God] plunges instead into a magnificent verbal tour of the natural world. He seems to guide Job through a private gallery of his favorite works, lingering with pride over dioramas of mountain goats, wild donkeys, ostriches, and eagles, speaking as if astonished by his own creations.[5]

Finally, Job responds to God, saying "My ears had heard of you, but now my eyes have seen you" (42:5). Before the whole ordeal, Job's relationship with the Lord existed and he was righteous. He knew God but maybe it was primarily through song and the words of his elders. Somehow the relationship was much more distant. Then through his trials came a new and profound intimacy with the Lord. With his own eyes, he now saw God in a more profound way!

The "Death Valley" Curve

Entrepreneurship has its own "valley" experiences. Bringing an innovative concept to market necessitates overcoming mountains of effort and challenges. There are product refinements, prototyping, strategic positioning, market research, hiring employees, customer identification, production, and marketing, among other things. The required financial resources can be substantial before you even make a dime.

This timeframe from the launching of a venture to the actual generation of revenue from early sales is commonly known as Death Valley or the Valley of Death Curve.[6] Prior to the actual generation of revenue via product sales, financial investors in new startups use this curve to project how much money is needed and the timing of those needs. A big question for startups is how much money they

will bleed before taking in revenue. When an innovation takes longer than expected or needs more money than projected, it puts the
venture in a particularly vulnerable position. Although the upside
is coming, some great discipline and hard sweat will be needed to
get to those financial rewards. Of course, some startups never make
it to the other side and fail someplace along the way.

The Death Valley Curve is indicative of the Christian life. And
even more foundational, it mirrors the life of Jesus. In his book
J-Curve, Paul Miller characterizes Jesus' life with the curves associated with the letter *J*. Jesus came to earth to live and then was
obedient to death, which was followed by his resurrection.[7] Jesus'
journey is emblematic with starting on the left-hand side of the
death curve, or the J-Curve, and culminating with Jesus' death. The
left-hand side starts by declining before it rises to new heights. Of
course, unlike our curves, Jesus' curve resolves the price of our sins
via his death at the bottom of his curve.

Figure 8.1. The "J-Curve"

While the curve of every new venture has its own unique
rhythm, the downward slope involves conquering various innovation and production problems if it's ultimately to be successful. As
followers of Jesus, the pain and suffering we endure kills or at least
weakens the darkness or evil within us. In this weakened state, we
move closer to Jesus and his resurrection power, which raises us
above where we started.[8]

Through pain comes God's higher purposes. He wants us to know his total sufficiency and the nearness of his presence. Pain and suffering are never easy, but they are a pathway to higher ground.

Pain and hardships have the potential to connect us to Jesus. He suffered through public judgment, ridicule, and the excruciating pain of the cross (e.g., John 18–19). Jesus is our example, and he becomes our hero when tough times come our way. In Colossians 1:24, Paul says, "Now I rejoice in what I am suffering for you, and I fill up in my flesh what is still lacking in regard to Christ's afflictions, for the sake of his body, which is the church."

When a piece of equipment breaks, when a false accusation damages your reputation, when partners break their promises—or something much worse—reluctant though you may be, engage with that downward cycle of the curve. Open your eyes so you can see God. Doing so will draw you toward God and lay the groundwork for your eventual resurrection.

Opportunities for Soul Work in Your Valleys of Death

While workplace pains and frustrations are never easy, embedded within them are opportunities for deeper growth with your God. Although your natural tendency is to run the other direction, stay the course, don't waste the pain.[9] We do have choices with how we respond. The next time you're on the downward side of the curve, there are constructive paths you can take. They will give you wonderful opportunities to bring about God's transforming presence in your life.

Retreats of Silence

The Gospels provide multiple accounts of Jesus frequently retreating from the crowds to pray, contemplate, and renew his perspective. For example, Luke 5:16 says that "Jesus often withdrew to lonely places and prayed." He used this time to commune with the Father, consider decisions, and keep his perspective aligned.

Suffering affects us emotionally. Our minds tend to get maxed out by trying to make sense of the dramatic event, and we have so many questions in this season. What an opportune time to retreat for an extended time of prayer and contemplation. Remember that God "shouts in our pain." Take time away from your mental overload and noise to capture the words of our Lord. If spending a day or more alone with God in a quiet place is new to you, then consider one of these resources: https://www.navigators.org/resource/spend-extended-time-prayer or https://intervarsity.org/blog/how-plan-retreat-silence.

The Upside of the Curve Is Coming

When you go through a painful period, there will be resistance distracting you from the resurrection side. First are the "why" questions. It seems to be a natural response, and we saw that Job had multiple "why" questions. God never answered Job's why questions, nor has he answered mine. While such questions can bury you, they can also be a gateway to grappling with your current reality. If you demand answers, however, this can lead you off the J-Curve to failure. While seeking to understand is a part of who we are, our minds are much too small to understand God's ways in any comprehensive manner.

Let God establish with you that the upside is coming. It's easy to set your eyes on the bottom of the curve and look for the end of your trial, but you don't own the timeline. Trials aren't so much about an endurance game. Rather, they are "all about who you know."[10] In Philippians 3:8–10, Paul says it powerfully:

> That I may gain Chris and be found in him . . . through faith in Christ—the righteousness that comes from God on the basis of faith. I want to know Christ—yes, to know the power of his resurrection and participation in his sufferings, becoming like him in his death.

Jesus was your forerunner, and he is already there in the hardships of your work, waiting on you. He longs for deeper companionship with you. To be more unified with Jesus is better than refined gold. It is the treasure is for all eternity!

Buddy It Up

When you get into the thick of a significant trial, don't go it alone. You're in uncharted waters, and you don't know the ending. You need a buddy with shared spiritual values with whom you can bare your soul. You need someone to pray with and to help you take your pains before the throne of grace. On the downhill side of the curve, you'll most likely find yourself without the words to utter the prayers of your heart. Your friend may then be able to pray for you, but you have even greater help: "The Spirit helps us in our weakness. We do not know what we ought to pray for, but the Spirit himself intercedes for us through wordless groans. And he who searches our hearts knows the mind of the Spirit, because the Spirit intercedes for God's people in accordance with the will of God" (Rom. 8:26–27).

The Parable of the Weeds

Jesus told them another parable: "The kingdom of heaven is like a man who sowed good seed in his field. But while everyone was sleeping, his enemy came and sowed weeds among the wheat, and went away. When the wheat sprouted and formed heads, then the weeds also appeared.

"The owner's servants came to him and said, 'Sir, didn't you sow good seed in your field? Where then did the weeds come from?'

"'An enemy did this,' he replied.

"The servants asked him, 'Do you want us to go and pull them up?'

" 'No,' he answered, 'because while you are pulling the weeds, you may uproot the wheat with them. Let both grow together until the harvest. At that time I will tell the harvesters: First collect the weeds and tie them in bundles to be burned; then gather the wheat and bring it into my barn.' "

The central truth of this parable is that the kingdom of heaven is alive and present with us. Even though evil still abounds in our world, God's work in those of us who have accepted him is alive and well. At some future point, Jesus will gather and burn the weeds (evil); the destruction of evil is not our responsibility. In the meantime, those of us who follow Jesus won't be squashed or uprooted with the weeds (evil). By his strength, we can grow in becoming more like him and bear fruit.

Sometimes we feel our jobs would be so much easier if we could work for a Christian business or even a church, but there are major trials even in these places. The evil and wrongdoing around us are everywhere, and sometimes this can be overwhelming. Life is not fair. But our growth with Jesus need not be minimized by the presence of weeds. Someday, we will be face-to-face with Jesus in his house.

Below is my paraphrase of this parable reset in modern day entrepreneur language.

The kingdom of heaven is now present among us. An entrepreneur started his business with ten employees (the good seed) who also followed Jesus. But as the business grew, additional employees came on board who did not follow Jesus.

Soon the VP of operations came to the owner and asked, "Where did these employees filled with darkness (weeds) come from?"

"From the devil," replied the owner.

"Do you want me to get rid of them?" asked the VP.

"No," replied the owner. "If you get rid of the employees filled with darkness, you will destroy everything. Those of us who follow Jesus can continue to grow because the kingdom of God is already in us as shown in the ministry of Jesus and the Holy Spirit. Those filled with darkness will be judged later. After that, the good employees will be gathered up and brought to my mansion where everything will be perfect. Together we will share in the full rewards of all."

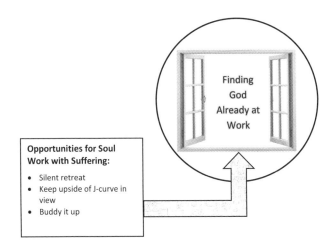

Chapter Model and Summary
Figure 8.2. The "Valley of Death" for Soul Work

Making sense of hard times in the workplace—whether they are physical, financial, emotional, or relational—is one of the biggest challenges we can face. Pain and suffering are results of the curse (see Gen. 3). Like Leslie in the opening scenario, the effects from the curse are widespread in all of our workplaces. This side of heaven, we can make only limited sense of the darkness of the workplace. But with the ministry of the Holy Spirit, we have the blessed opportunity to turn workplace hardships and challenges into significant soul work.

Your Next Steps

1. What is the biggest challenge you're currently dealing with in the workplace? Use the J-Curve to model this event.

2. Where does your view of suffering tend to get twisted? Is there something you need to ask the Holy Spirit for understanding?

3. Is there a passage of Scripture or a book referenced in this chapter that would be good for you to engage with further?

PART III

THE FRUIT OF BEING
WITH GOD AT WORK

9

AVODAH: WORSHIP AND WORK

Father of glory, it is a great honor and privilege to be in your presence. The more I discover your imprints in my work, the more I yearn for you. My most desired pleasure is expressing aspects of your presence with me. Impress on me how embedded in my work is with enjoying you more fully. You are the most glorious One. Open the eyes of my heart to see more of your presence in my work so I can more fully worship your greatness, beauty, and worth. Amen.

Avodah is my new favorite word! It has captivated me since I first learned of it. Widely used in the Old Testament, it's translated into English in three ways according to the context. "The word *avodah* means 'work and worship,' as well as 'service.'"[1] This Hebrew word expresses how God is interwoven with and gives great value to our work.

Avodah (or the root *avad* or *aved*) appears 145 times as a noun in the Old Testament.[2] It first appears in Genesis 2:15 where it is translated as "work": "The LORD God took the man and put him in the Garden of Eden to work it and take care of it." Here the context involves working the garden.

Second, *avodah* is often translated as "service" where one person submits to the allegiance of another. In 2 Samuel 16:19, we see an example of being subject to a king: "Furthermore, whom should I serve? Should I not serve the son? Just as I served your father, so I will serve you."

Finally, *avodah* is sometimes translated as "worship." This can be in reference to the worship of idols (Exod. 20:5) or worshiping YHWH. In Exodus 3:12, we read:

And God said, "I will be with you. And this will be the sign to you that it is I who have sent you: When you have brought the people out of Egypt, you will worship God on this mountain."

In God's design starting with the Garden of Eden, work and service and worship are brought together in a harmonious way.

Whether it is making bricks, crafting fine linen, or leading others in collective praise and worship, the Old Testament writers present a seamless understanding of work and worship. Though there are distinct nuances to *avodah*, a common thread of meaning emerges where work, worship, and service are intimately linked and intricately connected.[3]

Modern-day Jewish scholar Rabbi Ira F. Stone further reinforces the treble meaning of *avodah* when he says that "this is not an accident."[4] *Avodah* diminishes the common dichotomy between Sunday worship and Monday–Saturday work. As Tom Nelson says, "Our work has been designed by God to be an act of worship."[5]

A Journey of Work to Worship

Living in the intertwined nature of work and worship is wonderful, but it's a challenge to get beyond our tendency to keep them separated. I have wondered countless times about the extent of God's interest in my work. I so relish seeing God's thumbprint become evident in my work. But somehow, I also sensed I was just at the tip of the iceberg. Here are several of my noted work experiences with opportunities to personally connect with God.

- I am intrigued with the different kinds of wood used in building houses, constructing cabinets, exterior steps, etc. I still stand amazed that God would create so many different trees with such varied proprieties and uses. Whether for structural purposes or the way they absorb stain for aesthetics or for exterior weather conditions or for hardwood floors, different woods fill different purposes.

Response to God. While engaged with different woods vocationally, I barely realized they were signposts pointing me to God. However, my growing intrigue and understanding of wood was like a connector reminding me of how God was in my workday as well as in my Sunday worship.

- I was still transitioning into being an entrepreneurship professor when Bob, a senior colleague, walked in and said, "Hiring you was a great decision." With this new job, Bob had become a good friend as well as a colleague, mentor, and co-author. After being mostly alone professionally for several years, I clearly saw God's provision. My relationship with Bob changed the trajectory of my career.

Response to God. This was the fourth time a helpful mentor had come beside me, enabling a better pathway forward. God's gracious provision in this way was material for worship. I was grateful for Allen, Mark, Don, and then Bob for their timely input into my life. Unfortunately, I rarely let God's provision of these special men move me to honor him and his sovereignty in bringing these men into my life at just the right time.

- The university's entrepreneurship program was new, and several of our student teams had just won the top honors at an important business plan competition. These winnings were beneficial for the university, and they provided some clarification for our developing program. It also clarified for me some of my God-given giftings in working with students.

Response to God. I thanked God in my personal and family prayers, and I often credited God before others for these victories. In subsequent collective worship services, I recall thoughts of gratitude for this blessing from God. I wanted to lift praise to our God, but I had no idea how to do this in the service.

- Jake and I were appointed to build a program, but we had few guidelines and little accountability. While Jake and I shared a common goal, we rarely saw eye-to-eye on things. Our relationship was anything but smooth, and I needed help.

Response to God. I occasionally asked for prayer, but most of the time I was too intense with frustration and no apparent resolve. When some unexpected help came from a colleague, I blew right past his assistance because it was not in the form I thought best. Unfortunately, this relationship became a long-term burden to my "working" with God. Rarely did I let the challenges of this relationship connect me to God. It could have been a big draw to the foot of the cross. I squandered this opportunity.

Do you recognize God's thumbprints in your work? Jesus was called *Immanuel*, meaning "God with us" (Matt. 1:23). God is everywhere, which means that he is present with us in our work! He longs to connect with us more, much more! Where is God making his presence available to you in your work—maybe even in plain sight?

Pressing Toward Our Deepest Desires

As the deer pants for the streams of water, so my soul pants for you, my God. My soul thirst for God, for the living God. When can I go and meet with God? (Ps. 42:1–2)

Knowing God is the deepest and most foundational desire within us. Recognition of his imprint and presence in the central parts of our days and weeks are foundational for a deep response of adoration.

Worship is about responding to God and giving him the admiration and worth that is so rightfully his. When our minds become captivated by a fresh insight about God or when we sense a "God-touch," it's only natural to honor the giver and source of it. Worship is not something we manufacture or restrict to a specific time, but rather "is our responding to the overtures of love from the heart of the Father."[6]

When we discover God who is already at work in our innovations, our giftedness, and our struggles, we find ourselves with opportunities to connect with him. Our minds become captivated with our growing understandings of God, and then our "heart and affections are set on fire with joy and satisfaction and gratitude and gladness and admiration"[7] of who he is. Such worship is engaging with God and truly recognizing his greatness, beauty, worth, and goodness.

While genuine worship is a response, it does come in stages and there are things we can do to encourage it. Below I note the progression of four stages. The purpose here is to extend the "findings of God" at work that we covered in the previous five chapters. Stated differently, the stages of presence, seeing, learning, and the pinnacle of worship bring us to the deepest desires of our hearts.

Stage 1: Presence

We gaze through the "windows" of our workplace, recognizing that God is already present. "He is before all things, and in him all things hold together" (Col. 1:17). We have no premise for worship if we don't recognize God's supremacy. While we may not always feel God's presence, "the Lord is near" (Phil. 4:5) all the time.

Stage 2: Seeing

We need to ask God to drop the scales from our eyes to see him. Consider Paul's prayer that he will "give you the Spirit of wisdom and revelation, so that you may know him better. I pray that the eyes of your heart may be enlightened in order that you may know the hope to which he has called you, the riches of his glorious inheritance in his holy people" (Eph. 1:17–18). God, through the Holy Spirit, is the one who ultimately opens our eyes to see him.

Stage 3: Learning

All truth is God's truth, whether in words from the rock-solid Scriptures, from the various elements of creation with which we work, or through people made in his image. After God gave Daniel understanding and the interpretation of Nebuchadnezzar's dream, he responded to God, saying, "He gives wisdom to the wise and knowledge to the discerning. He reveals deep and hidden things; he knows what lies in darkness, and light dwells with him" (Dan. 2:21–22). When we connect with new revelations of truth through the work of our hands and minds, we are renewed in our praise of our great God.

The Pinnacle of Worship!

All honorable work can result in worship (*avodah!*), and so we can declare the greatness and worthiness of our God. What a joy for the work of our hands and minds that connect us to him. Yet, our "delight is incomplete till it is expressed."[8] Stated differently, "Enjoyment itself is stunted and hindered if it is never expressed in joyful celebration."[9] Therefore, in our private and collective worship, we give honor and praise to our God. Such expressions can touch us deeply. They also align us with the true north.

When we come to know God's creation and his presence underpinning the work of our hands and minds, he is thrilled. "God is most glorified in us when we are most satisfied in him."[10] God is joy-filled when we peer into the windows of the work of our hands and minds and recognize his abundant presence. Our work represents golden opportunities to engage with the creator and the owner of all.

Engaging Worship!

Building on chapters 4–8, the goal of this section is to help you arrive at specific worship. Joy-filled worship comes from gaining fresh insights and accomplishments in areas of your work where you now recognize his presence.

True worship is not secondhand. It comes from the connection between you and God. Building on the last five chapters where we discussed innovations, giftedness, loving our coworkers, injustices, as well as trial and hardships, the outline and questions below are intended to facilitate your own personal and intimate journey into worshiping your God. From major successes and challenges with work projects to workplace pains, God longs for us to connect with him.

From Innovation to Worship (Chapter 4)

Stage 1: The Presence of God in Innovation

Give recognition to God the Creator who is everywhere present. His thumbprints are in the iron, rubber, chemicals, the order represented in mathematics and programing code, plant and animal life, electricity, water, sun, oil, and so on. Through what elements are you closest to reflecting the God who is there?

Stage 2: Seeing God in Innovative Pursuits

Perhaps you have pondered inventors who came before you in developing one of your building blocks such as combustible engines, semi-conductors, the processing of different plants for food or medicinal purposes, or the milling of steel in the machines on which you build.

Are there unique insights that God is giving you about how A leads to B or how B leads to M, dots that no one else has previously connected?

Stage 3: Learning More of God in the Innovation

One of the reasons why innovation is so conducive to finding and experiencing God is because it requires further learning. If X responds to Y under one set of circumstances but not another, why? Therein invariably lies multiple opportunities to learn more about the complexities and intricacies coming from the Creator.

Stage 4: Responses of Worship from Your Innovative Pursuits

As the Spirit draws your attention to one or more phenomena of creation related to an innovation with which you are working, ponder it further. Offer praise to God for his truth in the complexities and intricacies in which he is allowing you to participate in and perhaps enabling you to have further insights.

From Giftedness to Worship (Chapter 5)

Stage 1: The Presence of God in Your Giftedness

"For you created my inmost being; you knit me together in my mother's womb. I praise you because I am fearfully and wonderfully made" (Ps. 139:13–14). This includes your giftedness and skills that God has given you to accomplish your work every day.

Stage 2: Seeing God in Your Giftedness

When we use our giftings, we usually get new glimpses with greater depth into some aspect of who God is and what he has created. Can you articulate the unique insights in which God is also opening your eyes?

Stage 3: Learning More of God in Your Giftedness

The more you learn of the subtle nuances and effectiveness of functioning in your giftedness, the more you learn about the nature of God.

Stage 4: Responses of Worship through Giftedness

After Daniel prayed to God to know Nebuchadnezzar's dreams, he praised God saying: "He gives wisdom to the wise and knowledge to the discerning. He reveals deep and hidden things" (Dan. 2:22–23). Daniel already had significant wisdom and knowledge, but then God gave him more. This resulted in Daniel's abundant expression of joy and praise.

Loving Your Neighbor Becoming Worship (Chapter 6)

Stage 1: The Presence of God in Loving Your Neighbor

God can be in the people he brings across your pathway. Consider again the story of the good Samaritan coming to the aid of the traveler who had been attacked. Who is God bringing across your pathway? Is it someone getting a bad rap because of past mistakes? Is it someone encountering an illness or the loss of a family member?

Stage 2: Seeing God in Loving Your Neighbor

Given that God cares deeply about our neighbors, especially those who have fallen on hard times, reaching out to them is an opportunity to see God in action before our very eyes. Given that all people are made in God's image, his "face" can be seen in others. Reaching out to our neighbors opens our personal windows to the winds of the Spirit.

Stage 3: Learning More of God in Loving Your Neighbor

As you connect to others, watch for God. This is a big opportunity to learn about yourself, about other people, and, most of all, about God.

Stage 4: Responses of Worship through Loving Your Neighbor

Come with gratitude before God for the privilege of being able to work with others as well as being a light to them. When the heart of your neighbor is met by God and you get a small opportunity to support, enrich, or ennoble that neighbor, your heart will be drawn to worship.

From Injustices to Worship (Chapter 7)

Stage 1: The Presence of God through Injustices

Despite the pending arrival of the ruthless Babylonians, Habakkuk says, "Though the fig tree does not bud and there are no grapes on the vines . . . and no cattle in the stalls, yet I will rejoice in the Lord, I will be joyful in God my Savior" (Hab. 3:17–18). Injustices have their own way of leading us to cry out to God.

Stage 2: Seeing God in Injustices

Exposing ourselves to needs can sensitize us to seeing God and his justices. Find one or more places to advocate for justice in your workplace.

Stage 3: Learning More of God in Injustices

Offer dignity to others as God brings dignity to those of us who seek him. Might you build a venture from your God-given gifts and entrepreneurial capabilities to address a specific injustice? What can you learn about God through the injustices in your workplace?

Stage 4: Responses of Worship through Injustices

"The Sovereign Lord is my strength; he makes my feet like the feet of a deer, he enables me to tread on the heights" (Hab. 3:19). God desires to make your feet like that of a deer, even when injustices surround you.

Pain as a Pathway to Worship (Chapter 8)

Stage 1: The Presence of God in Your Pain

"Even though I walk through the darkest valley, I will fear no evil, for you are with me; your rod and your staff, they comfort me" (Ps.

23:4). God's presence can become particularly evident in the valleys. Let your workplace challenges and pains bring you to the feet of Jesus.

Stage 2: Seeing God in Your Pain

In looking back on his tough season, Job noted that previously his ears had heard of God, but now his eyes have seen God (Job 42:5). Hardships and trials have a way of opening our eyes to things we couldn't see before.

Stage 3: Learning More of God in Your Pain

Hardships are the great teacher and have a way of leading us to rethink what we previously thought to be true. What is God teaching you through your hardship?

Stage 4: Responses of Worship in Pain

- After over four hundred years of slavery and the dramatic escape from Pharaoh through the Red Sea, Moses and the Israelites sang, "I will sing to the Lord, for he is highly exalted. Both horse and driver he has hurled into the sea. The Lord is my strength and my defense; he has become my salvation" (Exod. 15:1–2).

- Worship is often a spontaneous response to tragedy. In Job's unexpected surge of losses, he says, "Naked I came from my mother's womb, and naked I will depart. The Lord gave and the Lord has taken away; may the name of the Lord be praised" (Job 1:21). When you are in a "valley," try crying out to the Lord as a way of releasing your pain to him.

Which of the above sections resonate most with you? Or perhaps there is another area stemming from your work not developed in this book. Ask the Spirit to peel back the layers of your onion so that you may worship him in truth and in spirit.

Incarnation, Work, and Worship

"I was sitting at my computer writing a blog post the other day when an insight hit me," said Mike, a gifted writer who pastored for thirty years and is now an entrepreneur in the publishing business. "The insight came out of nowhere, and after I wrote it, I stopped for a while just to meditate on it."

The insight emerged while Mike was engaged in his business. He had studied and preached the "incarnation" many times. "Jesus was born with flesh and skin and looked like everyone else. God did this so everyone would understand him and not get freaked out by the Son of God living among them." Then this insight that came to Mike: "The process of writing our message or story must be *incarnational* in nature. In other words, we must write in a way that our audience can understand it and receive it. God was more committed to his audience—us—than he was in communicating his message."

The Spirit gave Mike this insight while he was utilizing his giftedness in his publishing business. This understanding is now being extended to me and many others, for which I am grateful. But no one is more impacted by this insight than Mike. His subsequent celebrations of Christmas and Jesus' incarnation just rose to a new level! Through his work of writing, Mike received a special God-touch that led to a "new song" before the throne of grace.

Avodah: Take 2

At the beginning of this chapter, I discussed how work, service, and worship are brought together in a harmonious way with the Hebrew term *avodah*. Not only does this word affirm God's design of bringing work and worship together, but it also suggests that work and worship are combined in such a way as to enrich the qualities of each other.

When we grow in seeing God in our work, it leads to worship at both the individual and congregant levels. Instead of showing up for church worship with our spiritual tank on empty, we arrive seeking to give fuller expression to the thumbprints and exposure to God in our work. When we bring these experiences to our collective worship services, we can bring fuller expression to our delights in God and his abundant presence.

In connecting with God through the ups and downs of our work week, we arrive at our worship services thirsting for more of God. Our collective worship gives form to coming to the foot of the cross, to come thirsty and hungry ready to be filled more with him. Constructive congregant worship invites us to bring all of our life—including our work—to the foot of the cross.

At our collective worship services, we delight in God being fully present along with his specific touches in our work week. We also leave our worship services with a renewed desire to open our eyes wider to see his goodness in all of life. *Avodah!*

In building on Piper's statement that "God is most glorified in us when we are most satisfied in him,"[11] I offer a revision with a work perspective: "God is most glorified in our work when we are most satisfied in recognizing, seeing, learning, and worshiping him." Worship expresses our joy in God and in the work that he has provided for us. The deepest longings of our heart are met when we "take delight in the Lord, and he will give you the desires of your heart" (Ps. 37:4).

10

PREPARING YOUR WAY FOR SOUL WORK

I kneel before you, Father God, from whom my identity comes. I pray that from your glorious and unlimited resources you will empower me through your Spirit. May Christ make his home ever more in me so that I can increasingly understand how wide, how long, how high, and how deep your love is for me. I long to be made complete with your love, because through it I am filled with the fullness of life and the power that comes from you. You, O God, can do immeasurably more than I can ask or imagine. To you belong all majesty, beauty, and worth for ever and ever! Amen.
(personalized paraphrase of Eph. 3:14–21)

It was 6:15 a.m. as I prayed, "Lord, thank you that you are with me. I want to know you better today. Guide me as I meet with Russ to estimate the materials on the new house bid for the Nelsons. Also, grant your protection as we position the rafters on this large garage today."

Although the details varied from day to day, this reflected my morning prayers as a contractor. I assumed Jesus cared about my work. This is why I prayed about preparing a bid and for protection. But somehow, I sensed God's design for work was much more central than I conceived.

Since the first page of this book, we have been unwrapping how our work can be a valuable catalyst for finding God. In part 1, we discussed the separation between work and faith that so often accompanies this discussion. Against this backdrop, I introduced a new paradigm and model in chapter 2: God is already at work! Furthermore, work provides great opportunities for deepening our spiritual walks. We also examined multiple Scriptures for understanding how our God is already in our work.

In part 2, building on the premise that God is already at work, I offered five work disciplines for opening our windows for the Spirit to move in us. These disciplines open up opportunities for us to touch, feel, taste, and smell our God who is already there. *Immanuel*—God is already with us, even in our work. This section developed the work disciplines of innovation, giftedness, loving our neighbors, pursuing justice, and engaging with hardships. These are also windows of opportunities to create potential pathways for God to connect with us.

Finally, part 3 addressed the fruit of being with God at work. Connecting with God at work brings our work and worship together—*avodah*! This is where work and worship become intertwined and inseparable. Worship can flow from real-life work experiences when we connect with God at work.

The final question we have been building toward is this: How might you prepare your way for meeting God who is already in your work? This last chapter puts into action the spiritual work disciplines we developed in chapters 4–8. Also offered are two examples: a modern-day case of "Jesus at the Joystick," and one from the Bible where Joshua connects with God in his work.

May God grant you new eyes to see your opportunities to participate in serious soul work through your work.

Why Work Disciplines Prepare the Way

"People have a body for one reason—that we might have at our disposal the resources that would allow us to be persons in fellowship and cooperation with a personal God."[1] Here, Dallas Willard is saying that we all have God-given abilities and freedoms to pursue either good pathways or destructive routes. We all have the option to be instrumental in shaping and reforming who we are.

Thanks to the work of people like Dallas Willard and Richard Foster, engaging with the spiritual disciplines is a means of transforming our character. The work disciplines discussed in this book are like resources for refurbishing our dry and broken souls that are too accustomed to living apart from God.

Unfortunately, our souls at work are typically like parched lands, void of anything spiritual. But this barren land can be watered and prepared for major flourishing. Engaging with the spiritual work disciplines is like digging irrigation channels through the barren section of land to make a way for water to flow to thirsty plants. The practice of the disciplines is like Jesus' living water flowing through our parched souls so that they can thrive.

This is great news! Our places of work offer us multiple opportunities to connect with the living God. Your work context is packed with many opportunities based on your God-given abilities, personality, and experiences. Exercising the spiritual work disciplines opens windows of collaborating and communing with God to connect with him more and forever. Spiritual disciplines are like pathways to the presence of Jesus among us. Or think of them as resources facilitating the building of our souls to connect us with our God who is already at work. They are pathways to the real presence of Jesus among us.

In the words of John the Baptist, "Prepare the way for the Lord; make straight paths for him" (Matt. 3:3). In other words, "A discipline for the spiritual life is . . . an activity undertaken to bring us into more effective cooperation with Christ and his Kingdom."[2] Work disciplines level our roads so that Jesus can enter into our lives.

We do not earn God's love by practicing spiritual disciplines. Nor are spiritual disciplines a yardstick for comparing ourselves to others. Rather, engaging the disciplines makes "us capable of receiving more of his life and power without harm to ourselves or others."[3]

What Work Disciplines Will You Pursue?

In chapters 4–8, we developed five disciplines for pursuing God in entrepreneurial workplaces. Practicing these disciplines enables the opening of the windows of our souls, so that by God's grace the winds of the Holy Spirit can blow on us.

In getting to some practical outcomes, let's first recap the spiritual disciplines of work we developed in the earlier chapters.

Innovation (Chapter 4)

- Commit to the discipline of listening when innovating: It's not so much about your ideas as it is about transforming the pain/needs of people for whom you are innovating.

- Passion: Seek solutions in the area(s) where God is giving you a passion.

- Build on knowledge, understanding, and insights: What foundational "raw materials" has God given you to innovate around? Discover God's imprint in your foundational materials.

- Organizing innovations: Preparing, assimilating resources, and organizing viable ideas into a new venture.

Giftings (Chapter 5)

- The discipline of learning by doing: Take note of the impact (or lack) on others of the services you offer.

- Know your strengths: Keep increasing your understanding of your strengths.

- Develop and further train your competencies.

- Give thanks to God for the intricacies of your giftedness: Find God's imprint in your human design and use it to praise him for being fearfully and wonderfully made.

Loving Those at Work (Chapter 6)

- Regularly (daily?) reach out with engaging conversation across your workplace "zones."

- Hurts and offenses will come; learn the discipline and gift of forgiveness.

- Find ways daily to be compassionate and generous with your time, mentoring, listening, and helping colleagues with their challenges. Offer prayers and encouragements.

Injustices (Chapter 7)

- Recognize God's ultimate ownership of what you have and be a steward of your resources to address at least one workplace injustice.

- Use injustices to learn of God's heart toward you and others. Carve out at least one way to be compassionate to others in your workplace.

- Use your entrepreneurial capabilities to address an injustice by building a social business.

Pain and Suffering (Chapter 8)

- When pain and suffering hit, let them draw you to the feet of Jesus. Consider taking a regular private retreat to connect with God and process the pain.

- Engage the discipline of the full J-Curve cycle; the road down to the valley can be challenging but the upside is coming.

- Let a challenging season draw you into regular prayer together with a friend to help you walk forward.

Which of the above practices is most likely to stir your heart with your work? Evaluate the above alternatives by placing each articulated discipline into one of three categories labeled as A, B, or

C. The "A" group are the top work disciplines you're willing to make a regular part of your life right now. Look for one or two (probably not more than three disciplines) for your "A" category and then invite the Holy Spirit to give you discernment.

Your "B" category represents disciplines that hold potential for you to engage with down the road. But first, integrate and master your "A" list. Your "C" category are those disciplines in which you don't see much potential in the foreseeable future.

If you long to connect with Jesus more deeply, then use one or more of the work disciplines to open the windows of your heart. Exercise the work disciplines for greater connection with God and richer fellowship with him.

Jesus at the Joystick

Xalavier Nelson Jr. is a BAFTA-nominated narrative director and game developer whose work has been featured on sites such as *PC Gamer*, *I Need Diverse Games*, *Critical Distance*, *Waypoint*, *Kotaku*, and *Rock Paper Shotgun*. Interested at an early age in video games, he started in the gaming industry as a journalist at the age of twelve while pretending to be an adult.

As a teenager, Xalavier came to personally know Jesus and was repeatedly amazed by the truths on the pages of Scriptures that jumped out at him. He then began exploring Christian video games, but he found them stuffy and uninspiring. More importantly, they didn't match the rich life he was seeing in Scripture.

Jay Tholen is the game developer who introduced Xalavier to making video games that express key faith principles. Having worked previously at a call center in Florida, he now lived in a trailer park with no prospects for his future. Then Jay developed a video game called *Dropsy*, showcasing a horrifying clown who expresses nothing but joy and love for the world around him.

After meeting Jay, Xalavier was of the first to play *Dropsy*. For the first time, he saw how game stories can bring truths from the Scriptures into real life. He was excited that he could exhibit the tenets of his faith and the realities of the gospel in a video game. Xalavier now says this realization "changed the direction of my life."[4]

He soon put on his entrepreneurial hat and started building video games that expressed some of the foundations of his faith. Today, through games such as *Hypnospace, Can Androids Pray,* and *An Airport for Aliens Currently Run by Dogs,* he continues to build games that pattern the behavior God that desires of us.

Xalavier's career track has radically changed his relationship with God, and his work as a game developer often feels like "the engine through which I feel I have had a conversation with God."[5] Taking the reality of the gospel and turning it into a game has become a way for him to internalize the good news and make the Bible increasingly real to him. *Jesus at the Joystick* is a victory!

Building video games that integrate biblical tenets into an adventure is a way of sharing himself with others. He even talks of developing a connection with the future players. He is practicing the discipline of listening in order to gain insights into what game players care about.

Particularly noteworthy is the impact that building video games is having on Xalavier's life with Jesus. His engagement with them pushes him to consider God's truth in new ways and how the world works in lieu of his reality. He continues to develop his God-given skills and capabilities to create even better games. In so doing, he is learning to appreciate the breadth of God's creation.

By developing his work disciplines of innovation and giftings, Xalavier is flourishing like many other entrepreneurs. Such disciplines open new opportunities to touch the lives of others for Jesus' name's sake.

Joshua's Battlefronts

In the fifth chapter of the book of Joshua, which I think is a remarkable passage, God has given Joshua the responsibility of leading the children of Israel into the promised land. They had already successfully crossed the Jordan River and were now to take control of the land city by city. Joshua's job is now a military leader preparing for his first major battle. Of all the cities, Jericho is the first target.

Now when Joshua was near Jericho, he looked up and saw a man standing in front of him with a drawn sword in his hand. Joshua went up to him and asked, "Are you for us or for our enemies?"

"Neither," he replied, "but as commander of the army of the Lord I have now come." Then Joshua fell facedown to the ground in reverence, and asked him, "What message does my Lord have for his servant?"

The commander of the Lord's army replied, "Take off your sandals, for the place where you are standing is holy." And Joshua did so. (Josh. 5:13–15)

Joshua is dealing here with a couple of battlefronts, visible and invisible. The visible one is Jericho, which stands right in front of him with its great wall. The invisible one is most likely his timidity and thoughts of being underqualified for this task. Given the setting and the man who was suddenly standing in front of him, I'm surprised Joshua had the wherewithal to ask: "Are you for us, or for our adversaries?" He was not by the Ark of the Covenant where God's voice was most expected (Num. 7:89). He was not at a Passover celebration.

In contemplating Joshua's battlefront, I wonder how many times I've looked past God who was already on the frontline of my workplace. The Lord set up Joshua's job as general of his army to communicate his next step, and the workplace turned out to be a potent context to do so.

Likewise, we need to consider that often the Lord also uses our workplaces to communicate his purposes. Frankly, I wonder how many times I've met up with an angel only to blow right by.

Joshua also was brave enough to inquire what the Lord has to say to him. What a great response. How often do I ask the Lord, "Is there a message you have for me?" When I have a breakthrough idea, am overwhelmed or uncertain about which way to go, wounded by others, or an unexpected turn of events alters my course, I need to remember to ask, "What message does my Lord have for his servant?"

Touching and Being Touched by God

Being "touched" by God is the deepest and most satisfying joy of our lives, and where we commonly spend forty to sixty hours a week holds an abundance of opportunities for connecting with God. The paradigm offered in this book has been suggesting that God is already in your work and wants to connect with you. Engagement with innovation, giftedness, loving others at work, injustices, and work pains are designed to open up new frontiers in your spiritual journey. Insights from the Scriptures, as well as personal examples like Xalavier's, point us in this direction.

Now it's your turn. Because you're uniquely and wonderfully made, the real potential of your journey with God is between you and him. The nuances of your giftings and why certain interests and experiences resonate with your soul defies standardization. When you personally understand and relish the capabilities and perspectives our Lord has implanted in you for utilization in the workplace, profound joy awaits your soul! You need to unwrap and personalize your own journey—no one can do it for you. Open your unique pathways at work for connecting with our Lord. Start with pursuing one or more work disciplines and discover God who is already at your workplace. Come to know his touches in your work by the power of the Holy Spirit.

As you start practicing your work disciplines, consider asking yourself these five questions to help launch your journey:

1. What specific work discipline would God have me practice to better connect with him?

2. With whom will I practice this work discipline? When should I start when, and how often will we meet (hourly, daily, weekly)?

3. How is the Holy Spirit working in my life? How can God send the Spirit into my "window"?

4. How can I commit to making a regular time once a day/week to contemplate how God may be present and even touching me in my work?

5. What further understanding or training could I pursue to further fine-tune and extend this work discipline as a channel for connecting with God?

Conclusion via the Parable of the Barren Fig Tree

Then [Jesus] told this parable: "A man had a fig tree growing in his vineyard, and he went to look for fruit on it but did not find any. So he said to the man who took care of the vineyard, 'For three years now I've been coming to look for fruit on this fig tree and haven't found any. Cut it down! Why should it use up the soil?'

"'Sir,' the man replied, 'leave it alone for one more year, and I'll dig around it and fertilize it. If it bears fruit next year, fine! If not, then cut it down.'" (Luke 13:6–9)

This barren fig tree parable is immediately preceded by Jesus discussing the tower over the pool of Siloam that unexpectedly fell and killed eighteen people. The point Jesus was making is "but unless you repent, you too will all perish" (Luke 13:5). With the parable of the barren fig tree, Jesus is making this same point.

This parable has three entities: (1) the vineyard owner represents God who expects to see fruit on his trees; (2) the vineyard keeper or gardener represents Jesus who oversees the watering, pruning, and fertilizing of the trees; and (3) the fruit on these trees or the lack thereof represents individuals.

Here is my paraphrase of the parable within an entrepreneurial setting:

God took a small grouping of his resources to build a nursery business. Several years later, he went to check in on how it was doing. Unfortunately, an investment in a unique tree had yet to bear any fruit. So he said to Jesus, who oversaw the business, "This is the third year I've come to check on this tree. I have yet to see any sales and return. Let's close this part of the business and sell off the assets. I have better places to use these resources." Being a compassionate gardener, Jesus pleaded for one more year to give more time and input for this tree to respond, to come to repentance. Maybe with a few more strategically placed life incidents, this entrepreneur will fall on his knees, repent of his wrongful pursuits, and look to Jesus to water and fertilize his soul and make it flourish. So he says to the Father, "If he doesn't repent and look to me for his resources within one more year, then cut him down."

The tree in this parable is alive but not going anywhere. In a similar way, you're obviously alive, but are you willing to bear fruit for the kingdom of God in your work? Is your work moving you forward in your spiritual journey with Jesus? Do you understand that the ultimate purpose of your work is to grow and bear fruit?

We have all squandered many opportunities in our work lives. But here is the question of the hour: Are you ready to meet God who is already there in your work, waiting for you to take off your blinders? Will you come before God with your wrong and unproductive roads? The pathway to a truly flourishing life starts with confessing your sins to the One who can cancel your debt. Humble yourself before the God of the universe as a part of your journey and then prepare for some wonderful soul work. He longs to bring you into a flourishing life that can matter both now and for all eternity. Jesus is compassionately pleading for a little more time for you to respond to him.

May your soul be well.

Appendix for Pastors

How to Help Your Congregants Engage with Soul Work

1

Sunday to Monday +
Monday to Sunday

Many people of faith understand that God is omnipresent, at least in theory. In practice, however, most people don't feel his presence—particularly at work. The central objective of this book has been to show that God is already present in the workplace and longs to connect with us there. Furthermore, with our work comes many opportunities to engage with soul work.

Most faith and work discussions fall into the "Sunday to Monday" framework. A worthwhile image involves Sunday services filling our cups. Then congregants can draw from their Sunday fillings throughout their workweek; but by Friday, most are already on empty and need to refill again on Sunday. Sunday services invite us in to drink of the living water to gain refreshment and to eat of the bread of life. Seeking to give congregants a "spiritual meal" on Sunday is right and honoring to our Lord. We all need our nourishment.

But our worship services can be so much more! When worshipers gather on Sunday, what if they could bring at least some of their experiences from their workweek? What if congregants came to our services cognizant of their God sightings in their workplace? If congregants have had a knee-dropping event in their work, whether it was from a humbling failure or recognition of a success with roots far beyond anything they did, wouldn't it be life-changing for them to bring that awareness into our collective worship?

I contend that this would open many doors for congregants to flourish with life seven days a week. This is illustrated in Figure A below. The top half is the Sunday to Monday Model. Here, Sunday is viewed as the day congregants are filled spiritually and then draw on this filling during the workweek. There is truth to this model, but it is incomplete.

The Monday to Sunday Model is shown on the bottom half of Figure A. The message of this book says the workplace also has the potential to offer an abundance of opportunities to deepen our spiritual journey. Furthermore, Sunday worship isn't a one-way street. Workers bring to our collective worship their God touches in the form of struggles, successes, new opportunities, and burdened hearts. This is a living out of *avodah* (as discussed in chapter 9) when work and worship come together and become interwoven.

Not only are we commanded to continue to come together in community, but we need one another to be spurred on in our faith. We all need to be filled. And as a part of a more complete filling, congregants need space to bring their workplace experiences into communal worship. If they check their workplace experiences at the door, it puts the squeeze on a major artery into which God intends to breathe life.

Sunday worship should involve both bringing and taking. For starters, congregants can be invited to bring their workweek experiences into prayers, songs, conversations, and offerings. They can offer nourishment through teaching, liturgy, song lyrics, participation in the sacraments, and visiting with others.

But there is more. How do we invite workweek experiences into our worship? How do we create more of a give-and-take worship? God is already at work wanting us to connect with him there. As we join with God in the workplace, our souls start to flourish, and we want to worship him. Our everyday work gives energy for Sunday worship.

"Work" to Energize Sunday Worship

When workers arrive at worship gatherings after at least some connecting with God in their workweek, they will most likely be unable to detach from those connections. The stage is set for a service involving both bringing and receiving.

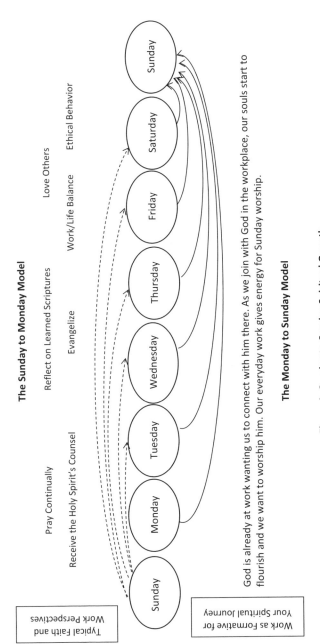

Figure A. Sunday to Sunday Spiritual Growth

Let's consider the mindset of a congregant who has experienced one or more God touches during their work week. Maybe they had a breakthrough insight on an innovation they had been grappling with for a while. Or maybe it was a particularly constructive conversation with a coworker or a problem that keeps getting deeper with no apparent end.

If they're already finding God at work, then such experiences are likely to trigger an individual response of thanksgiving and seeking our God. Since "true worship is a valuing or treasuring of God above all things,"[1] it's a matter of the heart, and a heart of worship starts with what's inside. Worship is a response to our awareness of God's great worth. I refer here to privately expressed worship as Level 1 Worship.

But our own private worship is only partially satisfying. It takes a community to give full expression to our worship, which I refer to as Level 2 Worship. Let me illustrate with the example of watching my favorite team score the winning touchdown in the final seconds. If I'm by myself, I may not be totally passive, but it also won't be an all-out celebration. If I'm with other like-minded fans, however, then our loud yells with high-fives and team chats come together in one big collective celebration and the energy flows.

Worship expresses our joy in God and in the work that he's provided for us. "Enjoyment itself is stunted and hindered if it is never expressed in joyful celebration."[2] Thus, when we experience those God touches in the workplace, finding further expression in a collective service deepens the worship experience. Furthermore, this fuller expression of thanksgiving and worship enables a fuller processing of the God touches experienced.

When congregants bring their workplace connections with God into our collective worship, everyone gains. At the individual level, it opens workers to be able to further process where their work fits into God's bigger story. Collective affirmation is a connection made through song, liturgy, Scripture, personal sharing, giving, and so on. Such fuller expressions of joy in God take us to Level 2 Worship.

When workers are invited to bring their God touches from their workweek into our collective worships, they enliven the fuller worship. Furthermore, doing so opens the door wider for workers to integrate the biblical truths that are being offered in our services. We then leave our collective worship services with a filling and impetus to enter our new workweek with renewed desire to be the goodness of God to others.

In their book *Work and Worship: Reconnecting Our labor and Liturgy*, Matthew Kaemingk and Cory Willson focus on rethinking Sunday in the light of work and workers.[3] These authors bring work and collective worship together by showing how both work and worship need to inform and impact each other. They offer numerous ideas and scenarios for worship services that will encourage congregants. This is an important read for those interested in leading workers into worship.

I also highly recommend the book *Every Job a Parable: What Walmart Greeters, Nurses and Astronauts Tell Us about God* by John Van Sloten. Pastor Van Sloten, who considers his own work in "The Parable of a Pastor," says that his "greatest vocational joy is bearing witness to God's everywhere presence so that others can do the same."[4]

2

Pastors and Entrepreneurs Helping One Another

It seems that both pastors and entrepreneurs often don't understand one another very well, although the reality is that we all need each other. This section is designed to help pastors better understand entrepreneurs, followed by how entrepreneurs can likewise be of value to pastors.

How Entrepreneurs Need Pastors

Entrepreneurship Is a Lonely Pursuit

The lonely road is true for most leaders, including pastors. It's also true for entrepreneurs. Entrepreneurship is about going against the grain to bring a new solution to an undeveloped market. It's also about dealing with frequent rejections from investors and potential clients. For starters, consider the following questions in your conversation with an entrepreneur:

- What kind of innovation are you pursuing?
- Where does your business go against the norms of competitors?
- Where are your biggest rejections currently coming from?
- Who do you go to when your back is against the wall?

God Is Already in Their Work and Values It

One of the best ways to affirm an entrepreneur is to show an interest in and value their work. First, seek to understand their business at least at a broad level. As a pastor, your attempts to understand their business and its contribution to employees, customers, and the common good of a community will speak volumes. Your questions and initiatives in this direction will do much to break down the sacred-secular divide.

- In what part of your work are you discovering more about God?

- In what ways is your work like a parable that reveals a deeper truth about God?[1]

- How is your work contributing to your own spiritual journey?

- In what ways is your work/company contributing to the lives of others and the common good?

Their Giftedness at Work

Many Christians seem to feel that their God-endowed giftedness is relevant only within the household of faith. The reality is that their very own business is undoubtedly anchored their giftedness. Their "eyes" to see a specific need or gap around which their innovation is built most likely emerged out of some of those unique gifts. Discuss with them their giftedness as utilized in the workplace.

- How are your unique gifts most evident in the innovation you've pursued?

- How are your unique gifts most evident in the business you're building?

- How are you compensating for areas in which you're not gifted? (Entrepreneurship requires being a Jack of many trades but working in area where they're not gifted most likely brings tension and lack of fulfillment.)

Work Demands and Relationships

There are many seasons in an entrepreneurial journey when demands are high and deadlines must be met. Limited resources and growth aspirations often require long hours. Inquire about their relational support and where "holes" exist.

- What are the biggest demands on your time?

- How do your spouse and children feel about your business?

- How do you make up for a busy season afterwards with your family?

- Where have you done best with work-life balance issues? Where do you struggle?

Dealing with Success

If an entrepreneur in your congregation has been successful but has recently sold their business, you should look for warning signs that something may be heading in the wrong direction. The fame of a successful venture and the proceeds from a buyout are likely to leave them feeling self-sufficient and that they can probably self-fund virtually anything they want. At the same time, such individuals are usually in a vulnerable position.

- What is the next significant contribution you seek to make with your life?

- Given your fame and wealth, where are you vulnerable?

- Is there a social entrepreneurial venture to be started as an outreach connected to the church?

How Entrepreneurs Can Help Pastors

Entrepreneurs are a unique subset of business leaders with some amazing skills and capabilities (as we discussed in chapter 5). They are typically high-energy individuals who rarely see a challenge with which they don't want to engage. On the other hand, most churches tend to be more stable with changes coming gradually. However, if a church is going to flourish, change needs to be embraced.

The church today is "desperately missing the gift of spiritual entrepreneurship."[2] The creative approaches of entrepreneurs for addressing emerging challenges can be of great value to pastors as they lead their churches. Below I address some ways pastors might consider utilizing some of the entrepreneurial talents in their church.

Bring Entrepreneurial Thinking into Your Church

Entrepreneurial thinking takes troubling and changing circumstances to creatively pursue new possibilities to better serve those whom God is leading your way. Troubling circumstances can disrupt what has historically worked. The temptation is to think this is the end of an era or dwell on how things are just not the way they use to be. However, entrepreneurial thinking brings a mindset that considers the broader context. A changing context almost always brings with it new opportunities, so what are the new alternatives that need to be developed?

Bring in people with an entrepreneurial background to help build your organization. Maybe your elder/leadership board could involve some individuals with such a mindset. It can also be helpful to have an entrepreneurial mindset present on your staff team or other committees in your organization.

Fix or Start a New Program

As our world changes, organizations struggle with keeping programs effective. There are times to question the status quo and times to fix what is broken. Many entrepreneurs would be honored to put their entrepreneurial giftedness to work in the church. Creative minds and actions can change the game and do so from a grass-roots level. Furthermore, entrepreneurs are often good at bootstrapping new products and programs.

Caveats and Limitations

Like all giftings, entrepreneurs don't come without limitations. Positively, they have a bias for action. But sometimes entrepreneurs can be too action oriented. Establish the right boundaries around a given project together with the right team, while giving them enough room to take the ball and run with it. Furthermore, most entrepreneurs are better at starting things than finishing. They can easily get bored once the project reaches a stable level. Plan for succession and then put that entrepreneur to work on the next project.

3

SERMON SERIES ON GOD AND WORK

The importance of work in the development of our journey with God gets very little attention from our pulpits. In one of the earliest books on faith and work, Doug Sherman reported a study he conducted in which he polled "about 2,000 people who call themselves Christians and who regularly attend church. We asked each of them, 'Have you ever in your life heard a sermon, read book, listened to a tape, or been to a seminar that applied biblical principles to everyday work issues?' More than ninety percent replied no.'"[1] These numbers are alarming. Given the emergence of the faith and work movement over the past couple of decades, I hope these numbers have improved. But the point remains: Congregants long to hear from the pulpit how their faith fits with their work.

Below I outline some sermon series ideas on God in the workplace, which I hope will get you started with offering at least one or two.

Series Alternative I

Sermon 1: "What Does God Think About Work?"

Start with laying a biblical foundation for work. Genesis 1–3 is a great place to start. See chapter 3 of this book for an overview of this section of Scripture.

Sermon 2: "The Work Disciplines for Connecting to God in the Workplace"

The place of spiritual disciplines is to open our windows so the winds of the Holy Spirt can blow on us (see *Spirit of the Disciplines* by Dallas Willard and *Celebration of the Disciplines* by Richard Foster). Then consider picking one of the five spiritual work disciplines developed in chapters 4–8.

Sermon 3: "Work and Worship—Avodah!"

Work and worship come together in the Hebrew word *avodah*, which is frequently used in the Old Testament. Sometimes the word means "work," sometimes "service," and sometimes "worship." Worship can rightfully flow from our real-life work experiences because we have seen and been with the living God.

Sermon 4: "Preparing Your Work Pathway for the Lord"

Prepare your way for meeting God who is already at your work, like John the Baptist prepared the way of our Savior (Matt. 3). Make our paths straight by putting into action the spiritual work disciplines. Through God's resources, his fullness is available to fill up our spiritually parched hearts when we're at work. Possible passages include Ephesians 3:14–21.

Series Alternative II

Sermon 1: "What Does God Think about Work?"

Part 1. Biblical foundation for work: Genesis 1–3. Work was God's idea first. God created us with an ability to work and instructed Adam and Eve to work the garden. Then came the impact of the fall.

Part 2. In *Every Job a Parable,* John Van Sloten offers us a helpful look at how every job is like a parable that gives us further understanding into who God is.² God's revelation comes to us via creation. Select a congregant to interview and discuss how this individual's job has given them insight into the kingdom of God. Help them articulate how God's presence is in their work, offering a particular manifestation of who he is. Although it contains much merit, seek to get the conversation beyond an oral witness of the gospel at work.

Sermon 2: "The Wonders of God's Creation (Embedded in. Our Work)"

Part 1. Biblical foundation for work: Job 12:7–10; Proverbs 30:18–19; Matthew 6:26–29; Luke 6:48. As reflected in these verses, the thumbprints of God's creation can be observed in the trenches of our workplaces through soil, animals, foundations, or flood waters, and so on.

Part 2. Every Job a Parable (see note under Sermon 1/Part 2 of this series above).

Sermon 3: "Work Saved This Woman's Life"

Part 1. Biblical foundation for work: John 4:6–16. Jesus encounters the Samaritan woman in her work as a water gatherer. In and because of her work, he connects with her to reveal himself as the "living water."

Part 2. Every Job a Parable (see note under Sermon 1/Part 2 of this series above).

Sermon 4: "Mind-Bending Learning at Work with Jesus"

Part 1. Biblical foundation for work: Teach on one of Jesus' parables in which the story line is built around a work context. See Klaus Issler's article for further details.[3]

Part 2. Every Job a Parable (see note under Sermon 1/Part 2 of this series above).

Series Alternative III

Consider a multiple sermon series devoted to the parables of Jesus in which he builds his story line around a workplace issue. In addition to the parables used to conclude chapter 4–8 in this book, you could also consider the parable of the two builders (Matt. 7:24–27; Luke 6:47–49), the four soils (Matt. 13:3–9; Luke 8:5–8), the rich fool (Luke 12:13–21), the tower builder (Luke 14:28–30), and the unjust manager (Luke 16:1–13). Intentionally teach the sermon through the lens of the workplace and maybe do a transliteration of a current-day work context.

BIBLIOGRAPHY

"5 Reasons Millennials Stay Connected to Church." *The Barna Group* (September 17, 2013). https://www.barna.com/research/5 -reasons-millennials-stay-connected-to-church/.

Alvarez, Sharon A., and Lowell W. Busenitz. "The Entrepreneurship of Resource-Based Theory." *Journal of Management* (2001): 27:755–75.

"Audacious Love: How Daryl Davis Convinced 200 Racists to Leave the KKK." Video. The Veritas Forum, May 28, 2020. https:// www.youtube.com/watch?v=iuCyh_4E_mY.

Augustine of Hippo. *The Trinity*. Translated by Edmund Hill. Brooklyn, NY: New City Press, 1991.

Barney, Jay. "Looking Inside for Competitive Advantage." *Academy of Management Executive* 9, 49–61.

St. Bonaventure. *Itinerarium mentis ad Deum* (*The Works of St. Bonaventure*) 1.14. Edited by P. Boehner and Z. Hayes. St. Bonaventure, NY: Franciscan Institute, 2003.

Bornkamm, Heinrich. *Luther's World of Thought*. St. Louis: Concordia, 1958.

Busenitz, Lowell, and Jay Barney. "Differences between Entrepreneurs and Managers in Large Organizations: Biases and Heuristics in Strategic Decision Making." *Journal of Business Venturing* 12.1 (1997): 9–30.

Calvin, John. *Commentaries on the Epistles to Timothy, Titus, and Philemon*. http://classicchristianlibrary.org/library/calvin _john/Calvin-Tim_Tit_Phm.pdf.

———. *Institutes of the Christian Religion*. Edited by John T. McNeill. Translated by Ford Lewis Battles. Philadelphia: Westminster, 1960.

CB Insights. "The Top 12 Reasons Startups Fail." *Research Brief* (August 3, 2021). https://www.cbinsights.com/research /startup-failure-reasons-top/.

Cook, Ian. "Who Is Driving the Great Resignation?" *Harvard Business Review* (September 15, 2021). https://hbr.org/2021/09 /who-is-driving-the-great-resignation.

Corbett, Steve, and Brian Fikkert. *When Helping Hurts: How to Alleviate Poverty without Hurting the Poor and Yourself.* Chicago: Moody, 2009.

Daniels, Denise, and Shannon Vandewarker. *Working in the Presence of God: Spiritual Practices for Everyday Work.* Peabody, MA: Hendrickson, 2019.

Doriani, Daniel M. *Work: Its Purpose, Dignity, and Transformation.* Phillipsburg, NJ: P&R, 2019.

Eareckson Tada, Joni. *The God I Love: A Lifetime of Walking with Jesus.* Grand Rapids: Zondervan, 2003.

Ericsson, K. S., R. T. Krampe, and C. Tesch-Romer. "The Role of Deliberate Practice in the Acquisition of Expert Performance." *Psychological Review* 100, no. 3 (1993): 363–406.

Eusebius. *The Proof of the Gospel.* Translated by W. J. Ferrar. New York: Macmillan, 1920.

Fernando, Jason. "Death Valley Curve." Investopedia (July 16, 2021). https://www.investopedia.com/terms/d/death-valley -curve.asp.

Foster, Richard J. *Celebration of Discipline: The Path to Spiritual Growth.* 3rd ed. New York: HarperCollins, 2000.

Fujimura, Makoto. *Art and Faith: A Theology of Making.* New Haven: Yale University Press, 2020.

Gladwell, Malcolm. *Outliers: The Story of Success.* New York: Little, Brown, 2008.

Hasso Plattner Institute of Design at Stanford University. "Get Started with Design Thinking." https://dschool.stanford. edu/resources/getting-started-with-design-thinking.

Holmes, Arthur. *All Truth Is God's Truth.* Grand Rapids: Eerdmans, 1977.

Huber, Dave. "*Avodah* Word Study: Unpacking the Hebrew Verb 'to worship.'" *EFCA Today* (Summer 2012). http://www.efcatoday.org/story/avodah-word-study.

Issler, Klaus. "Exploring the Pervasive References to Work in Jesus' Parables." *Journal of the Evangelical Theological Society* 57.2 (2014): 323–39.

Kaemingk, Matthew, and Cory B. Willson. *Work and Worship: Reconnecting our Labor and Liturgy.* Grand Rapids: Baker Academic, 2020.

Keller, Timothy. *Generous Justice: How God's Grace Makes Us Just.* New York: Dutton, 2010.

Keller, Timothy, with Katherine Leary Alsdorf. *Every Good Endeavor: Connecting Your Work to God's Work.* New York: Penguin, 2012.

Kelley, Tom, and David Kelley. *Creative Confidence: Unleashing the Creative Potential within Us All.* New York: Crown, 2013.

Kelly, Jack. "Indeed Study Shows That Worker Burnout Is at Frighteningly High Levels: Here Is What You Need to Do Now." *Forbes* (April 5, 2021). https://www.forbes.com/sites/jackkelly/2021/04/05/indeed-study-shows-that-worker-burnout-is-at-frighteningly-high-levels-here-is-what-you-need-to-do-now/?sh=6704a52c23bb.

Lai, Patrick. *Workship: Recalibrate Work and Worship.* Mt. Clemens, MI: OPEN Worldwide, 2021.

Lee-Barnewall, Michelle. *Surprised by the Parables: Growing in Grace through the Stories of Jesus.* Bellingham, WA: Lexham Press, 2020.

Lewis, C. S. *The Problem of Pain.* New York: Harper, 2001.

———. *Reflections on the Psalms.* New York: Harcourt, Brace & Co., 1958.

Luther, Martin. "Lectures on Genesis." *Luther's Works.* Translated by Jaroslav Pelikan. St. Louis: Concordia, 1970.

Lyons, David, and Kathy Lyons Richardson. *Don't Waste the Pain: Learning to Grow through Suffering.* Colorado Springs: NavPress, 2010.

Miller, David W. *God at Work: The History and Promise of the Faith at Work Movement*. Oxford: Oxford University Press, 2006.

Miller, Paul E. *J-Curve: Dying and Rising with Jesus in Everyday Life*. Wheaton, IL: Crossway, 2019.

Morin, Rich, and Rakesh Kochhar. "The Impact of Long-term Unemployment." Pew Research Center. https://www.pew research.org/wp-content/uploads/sites/3/2010/11/760 -recession.pdf.

Nelson, Tom. *The Economics of Neighborly Love: Investing in Your Community's Compassion and Capacity*. Downers Grove, IL: IVP Books, 2017.

———. *Work Matters: Connecting Sunday Worship to Monday Work*. Wheaton, IL: Crossway, 2011.

Nelson Jr., Xalavier. "*Jesus at the Joystick*: Can Video Games be Spiritual?" Theology of Work Project (October 10, 2021). https://www.theologyofwork.org/makingitwork/episode /jesus-at-the-joystick-can-video-games-be-spiritual -xalavier-nelson-jr.

Nicolai de Cusa, *Defiliatione Dei*. *Nicolai de Cusa compendium* 8. Nicolaus Cusanus, Bruno Decker, and Karl Bormann. Hamburgi: in Aedibus Felicis Meiner, 1964.

Nieuwhof, Carey. "Why We Need More Entrepreneurial Church Leaders, Not More Shepherds." https://careynieuwhof .com/why-we-need-more-entrepreneurial-church-leaders -not-more-shepherds/.

Ornstein, Matthew, dir. *Accidental Courtesy: Daryl Davis, Race, and America*. First Run Features, 2017. DVD.

Pareto, Vilfredo. *Cours d'Économie Politique: Nouvelle édition par G.-H. Bousquet et G. Busino*. Geneva: Librairie Droz, 1964.

Peterson, Eugene H. *Christ Plays in Ten Thousand Places: A Conversation in Spiritual Theology*. Grand Rapids: Eerdmans, 2005.

Piper, John. "'All Truth Is God's Truth' Admits the Devil: Meditations on an Academic Slogan." https://www.desiringgod .org/articles/all-truth-is-gods-truth-admits-the-devil.

———. *Desiring God: Meditations of a Christian Hedonist*. Colorado Springs: Multnomah, 2011.

———. "What Is Worship?," *Desiring God* (blog). https://www.desiringgod.org/interviews/what-is-worship.

Raynor, Jordan. *Called to Create: A Biblical Invitation to Create, Innovate, and Risk*. Grand Rapids: Baker Books, 2017.

———. *Master of One: Find and Focus on the Work You Were Created to Do*. Colorado Springs: WaterBrook, 2020.

Roche, Bruno, and Jay Jakub. *Completing Capitalism: Healing Business to Heal the World*. Oakland, CA: Berrett-Koehler, 2017.

Sayers, Dorothy. *The Mind of the Maker*. San Francisco: Harper-Collins, 1968.

———. "Why Work? Marx and Human Nature." *Science & Society* 69.4 (2005): 606–16.

Sherman, Doug, and William Hendricks. *Your Work Matters to God*. Colorado Springs: NavPress, 1987.

"Spider Silk: Properties, Uses, and Production." http://www.chm.bris.ac.uk/motm/spider/page2.htm.

Stone, Ira F. "Service Is Work and Work Is Worship." *Reconstructing Judaism* (January 4, 2012). https://www.ritualwell.org/blog/service-work-and-work-worship-rabbi-ira-f-stone.

Storms, Sam. "Job Chapter 1." *Enjoying God* (blog). https://www.samstorms.org/all-articles/post/job-chapter-1 .

———. "Job Chapters 38–42." *Enjoying God* (blog). https://www.samstorms.org/all-articles/post/job-chapters-38–42.

———. "Praise: The Consummation of Joy." *I Love Praise and Worship* (blog). https://ilovepraiseandworship.net/2016/05/15/praise-the-consummation-of-joy/.

———. "Who Is My Neighbor? Wrong Question!" Bridgeway Church (May 8, 2011). Sermon. https://www.bridgewaychurch.com/sermons/sermon/2011–05–08/who-is-my-neighbor-wrong-question.

———. "Why Do We Sing for 30 Minutes at Bridgeway?" *Enjoying God* (blog). https://www.samstorms.org/enjoying-god-blog/post/why-do-we-sing-for-30-minutes-at-bridgeway.

Taylor, Justin. "10 Ideas Embedded in the Slogan 'All Truth Is God's Truth.'" *The Gospel Coalition.* https://www.thegospel coalition.org/blogs/justin-taylor/10-ideas-embedded -in-the-slogan-all-truth-is-gods-truth/.

Van Sloten, John. *Every Job a Parable: What Walmart Greeters, Nurses, and Astronauts Tell Us about God.* Colorado Springs: NavPress, 2017.

Wallace, J. Warner. "The Difference between 'Natural Talents' and 'Spiritual Gifts.'" *Cold Case Christianity* (July 5, 2019). https://coldcasechristianity.com/writings/the-difference -between-natural-talents-and-spiritual-gifts/.

Wenham, David. *The Parables of Jesus.* Downers Grove, IL: Inter-Varsity Press, 1989.

Whelchel, Hugh. *How Then Should We Work?* McLean, VA: Institute for Faith, Work & Economics, 2012.

Willard, Dallas. *The Divine Conspiracy: Rediscovering our Hidden Life in God.* San Francisco: Harper, 1997.

———. *The Spirit of the Disciplines: Understanding How God Changes Lives.* San Francisco: HarperOne, 1999.

Wingren, Gustaf. *The Christian's Calling: Luther on Vocation.* Edinburgh: Oliver & Boyd, 1958.

Wolters, Albert. *Creation Regained: Biblical Basics for a Reformational Worldview.* Grand Rapids: Eerdmans, 2005.

Yancey, Philip. *Disappointment with God: Three Questions No One Asks Aloud.* Grand Rapids: Zondervan, 1992.

"Young Invincibles Policy Brief: New Poll Finds More Than Half of Millennials Want to Start Businesses," Kauffman: The Foundation of Entrepreneurship. https://www.kauffman. org/wp-content/uploads/2020/06/young_invincibles _policy_brief_millennials.pdf.

Notes

Chapter 1

1. Tom Nelson, *Work Matters: Connecting Sunday Worship to Monday Work* (Wheaton, IL: Crossway, 2011), 44–45.

2. Martin Luther, "Lectures on Genesis," *Luther's Works*, trans. Jaroslav Pelikan (St. Louis: Concordia, 1970), 6:10; Gustaf Wingren, *The Christian's Calling: Luther on Vocation* (Edinburgh: Oliver & Boyd, 1958), 6–10.

3. John Calvin, *Institutes of the Christian Religion*, ed. John T. McNeill, trans. Ford Lewis Battles (Philadelphia: Westminster, 1960), 2.2.14–16 (273–75).

4. David W, Miller, *God at Work: The History and Promise of the Faith at Work Movement* (Oxford: Oxford University Press, 2006), 11.

5. Denise Daniels and Shannon Vandewarker, *Working in the Presence of God: Spiritual Practices for Everyday Work* (Peabody, MA: Hendrickson, 2019). See also Vandewarker and Daniels, *Practices for Working in the Presence of God: A Guided Journal* (Peabody, MA: Hendrickson, 2022).

6. Ian Cook, "Who Is Driving the Great Resignation?," *Harvard Business Review*, September 15, 2021, https://hbr.org/2021/09/who-is-driving-the-great-resignation.

7. "Young Invincibles Policy Brief: New Poll Finds More Than Half of Millennials Want to Start Businesses," *Kauffman: The Foundation of Entrepreneurship*, 2011, https://www.kauffman.org/wp-content/uploads/2020/06/young_invincibles_policy_brief_millennials.pdf.

8. Eugene H. Peterson, *Christ Plays in Ten Thousand Places: A Conversation in Spiritual Theology* (Grand Rapids: Eerdmans, 2005), 36.

9. Peterson, *Christ Plays in Ten Thousand Places*, 36–37.

Chapter 2

1. Arthur Holmes, *All Truth Is God's Truth* (Grand Rapids: Eerdmans, 1977).

2. John Calvin, *Commentaries on the Epistles to Timothy, Titus, and Philemon*, http://classicchristianlibrary.org/library/calvin_john/Calvin -Tim_Tit_Phm.pdf, accessed on February 11, 2022, 300–301.

3. Justin Taylor, "10 Ideas Embedded in the Slogan 'All Truth Is God's Truth,'" accessed February 9, 2022, https://www.thegospelcoalition.org /blogs/justin-taylor/10-ideas-embedded-in-the-slogan-all-truth-is-gods -truth/ (my italics).

4. John Piper, "'All Truth Is God's Truth' Admits the Devil: Meditations on an Academic Slogan" March 13, 2009, https://www.desiringgod .org/articles/all-truth-is-gods-truth-admits-the-devil.

5. Piper, "'All Truth Is God's Truth' Admits the Devil."

6. Peterson, *Christ Plays in Ten-Thousand Places*, 127.

7. Dallas Willard, *The Spirit of the Disciplines: Understanding How God Changes Lives* (San Francisco: HarperOne, 1999), 68.

8. Richard Foster, *Celebration of Discipline: The Path to Spiritual Growth* (New York: Harper, 2000), 7.

Chapter 3

1. Bonaventure, *Itinerarium mentis ad Deum* 1.14; Nicholas of Cusa, *Defiliatione Dei*, in *Compendium 8*.

2. Quoted in Heinrich Bornkamm, *Luther's World of Thought* (St. Louis: Concordia, 1958), 27.

3. John Van Sloten, *Every Job a Parable: What Walmart Greeters, Nurses, and Astronauts Tell Us about God* (Colorado Springs: NavPress, 2017), 36.

4. Klaus Issler, "Exploring the Pervasive References to Work in Jesus' Parables," *Journal of the Evangelical Theological Society* 57.2 (2014): 323–39.

5. Vilfredo Pareto, *Cours d'Économie Politique: Nouvelle édition par G. H. Bousquet et G. Busino* (Geneva: Librairie Droz, 1964).

6. Calvin, *Institutes*, 1.5.8; 1.14.20; 2.6.1.

Chapter 4

1. Spider Silk: Properties, Uses, and Production," accessed February 16, 2022, http://www.chm.bris.ac.uk/motm/spider/page2.htm.

2. Timothy Keller with Katherine Leary Alsdorf, *Every Good Endeavor: Connecting Your Work to God's Work* (New York: Penguin, 2012), 44.

3. Jordan Raynor, *Called to Create: A Biblical Invitation to Create, Innovate, and Risk* (Grand Rapids: Baker Books, 2017), 34.

4. Makoto Fujimura, *Art and Faith: A Theology of Making* (New Haven: Yale University Press, 2020).

5. Dorothy Sayers, *The Mind of the Maker* (San Francisco: Harper-Collins, 1968), 22.

6. Fujimura, *Art and Faith*, 6.

7. L. W. Busenitz and J. B. Barney, "Differences between entrepreneurs and managers in large organizations: Biases and heuristics in strategic decision making," *Journal of Business Venturing* 12.1 (1997): 9–30.

8. CB Insights, "The Top 12 Reasons Startups Fail," *Research Brief*, August 3, 2021, https://www.cbinsights.com/research/startup-failure -reasons-top/.

9. Hasso Plattner Institute of Design at Stanford University, "Get Started with Design Thinking," https://dschool.stanford.edu/resources /getting-started-with-design-thinking; Tom Kelley and David Kelley, *Creative Confidence: Unleashing the Creative Potential within Us All* (New York: Crown, 2013).

Chapter 5

1. Jordan Raynor, *Master of One: Find and Focus on the Work You Were Created to Do* (Colorado Springs: WaterBrook, 2020), xiii.

2. Raynor, *Master of One*, xiv.

3. J. Warner Wallace, "The Difference between 'Natural Talents' and 'Spiritual Gifts,'" July 5, 2019, https://coldcasechristianity.com/writings /the-difference-between-natural-talents-and-spiritual-gifts/.

4. Albert Wolters, *Creation Regained: Biblical Basics for a Reformational Worldview* (Grand Rapids: Eerdmans, 2005), 88.

5. Wolters, "Creation Regained," 88.

6. Jack Kelly, "Indeed Study Shows That Worker Burnout Is at Frighteningly High Levels: Here Is What You Need to Do Now," *Forbes* (April 5, 2021), https://www.forbes.com/sites/jackkelly/2021/04/05/indeed-study -shows-that-worker-burnout-is-at-frighteningly-high-levels-here-is -what-you-need-to-do-now/?sh=6704a52c23bb.

7. Raynor, *Master of One*.

8. Jordan Raynor, *Called to Create: A Biblical Invitation to Create, Innovate, and Risk* (Grand Rapids: Baker Books, 2017), 34.

9. Raynor, *Master of One*.

10. Keller with Alsdorf, *Every Good Endeavor*, 67.

11. Raynor, *Master of One*, xiv.

12. J. B. Barney, "Looking Inside for Competitive Advantage," *Academy of Management Executive* 9, 49–61; Sharon A. Alvarez and Lowell W. Busenitz, "The Entrepreneurship of Resource Based Theory," *Journal of Management* (2001), https://doi.org/10.1177/014920630102700609.

13. K. S. Ericsson, R. T. Krampe, and C. Tesch-Romer, "The Role of Deliberate Practice in the Acquisition of Expert Performance," *Psychological Review* 100, no. 3 (1993): 363–406.

14. Malcolm Gladwell, *Outliers: The Story of Success* (New York: Little, Brown, 2008).

Chapter 6

1. Sam Storms, "Who Is My Neighbor? Wrong Question!," Bridgeway Church, May 8, 2011 sermon, https://www.bridgewaychurch.com/sermons/sermon/2011-05-08/who-is-my-neighbor-wrong-question.

2. Storms, "Who Is My Neighbor?"

3. Michelle Lee-Barnewall, *Surprised by the Parables: Growing in Grace through the Stories of Jesus* (Bellingham, WA: Lexham Press, 2020).

4. *Accidental Courtesy: Daryl Davis, Race, and America*, directed by Matthew Ornstein (First Run Features, 2017), DVD.

5. *Accidental Courtesy.*

6. "Audacious Love: How Daryl Davis Convinced 200 Racists to Leave the KKK," *The Veritas Forum*, May 28, 2020, https://www.youtube.com/watch?v=iuCyh_4E_mY.

7. Dallas Willard, *The Divine Conspiracy: Rediscovering our Hidden Life in God* (San Francisco: Harper, 1997), 142.

Chapter 7

1. All names changed in this example.

2. Tom Nelson, *The Economics of Neighborly Love: Investing in Your Community's Compassion and Capacity* (Downers Grove, IL: IVP Books, 2017), 134.

3. Timothy Keller, *Generous Justice: How God's Grace Makes Us Just* (New York: Dutton, 2010), 82.

4. Keller, *Generous Justice*, 83.

5. Dorothy Sayers, "Why Work? Marx and Human Nature," *Science & Society* 69.4 (2005): 606–16.

6. Pew Research Center, "The Impact of Long-term Unemployment Lost Income, Lost Friends—and Loss of Self-respect," July 22, 2010, https://www.pewresearch.org/wp-content/uploads/sites/3/2010/11/760-recession.pdf.

7. Steve Corbett and Brian Fikkert, *When Helping Hurts: How to Alleviate Poverty without Hurting the Poor and Yourself* (Chicago: Moody, 2009).

8. Corbett and Fikkert, *When Helping Hurts*, 100.

9. Keller, *Generous Justice*, 126.

10. Bruno Roche and Jay Jakub, *Completing Capitalism: Healing Business to Heal the World* (Oakland, CA: Berrett-Koehler, 2017).

Chapter 8

1. Joni Eareckson Tada, *The God I Love: A Lifetime of Walking with Jesus* (Grand Rapids: Zondervan, 2003).
2. C. S. Lewis, *The Problem of Pain* (New York: Harper, 2001), 94.
3. Sam Storms, "Job Chapter 1," *Enjoying God*, https://www.samstorms.org/all-articles/post/job-chapter-1.
4. Sam Storms, "Job Chapters 38–42," *Enjoying God*, https://www.samstorms.org/all-articles/post/job-chapters-38–42.
5. Philip Yancey, *Disappointment with God: Three Questions No One Asks Aloud* (Grand Rapids: Zondervan, 1992), 212.
6. Jason Fernando, "Death Valley Curve," July 16, 2021, *Investopedia*, https://www.investopedia.com/terms/d/death-valley-curve.asp.
7. Paul E. Miller, *J-Curve: Dying and Rising with Jesus in Everyday Life* (Wheaton, IL: Crossway, 2019), 19.
8. Miller, *J-Curve*.
9. David Lyons with Kathy Lyons Richardson, *Don't Waste the Pain: Learning to Grow through Suffering* (Colorado Springs: NavPress, 2010).
10. Miller, *J-Curve*, 65.

Chapter 9

1. Miller, *God at Work*, 6.
2. Dave Huber, "*Avodah* Word Study: Unpacking the Hebrew Verb 'to worship,'" *EFCA Today* (Summer 2012), http://www.efcatoday.org/story/avodah-word-study; Patrick Lai, *Workship: Recalibrate Work and Worship* (Mt. Clemens, MI: OPEN Worldwide, 2021), 35–41.
3. Nelson, *Work Matters*, 26.
4. Rabbi Ira F. Stone, "Service Is Work and Work Is Worship," *Reconstructing Judaism*, January 4, 2012, https://www.ritualwell.org/blog/service-work-and-work-worship-rabbi-ira-f-stone.
5. Nelson, *Work Matters*, 27.
6. Richard J. Foster, *Celebration of Discipline* (San Francisco: Harper & Row, 1978), 138.
7. Sam Storms, "Why Do We Sing for 30 Minutes at Bridgeway?" *Enjoying God*, March 22, 2019, https://www.samstorms.org/enjoying-god-blog/post/why-do-we-sing-for-30-minutes-at-bridgeway.
8. C. S. Lewis, *Reflections on the Psalms* (New York: Harcourt, Brace & Co, 1958), 97.

9. Sam Storms, "Praise: The Consummation of Joy," I Love Praise and Worship, May 15, 2016, https://ilovepraiseandworship.net/2016/05/15/praise-the-consummation-of-joy/.

10. John Piper, *Desiring God: Meditations of a Christian Hedonist* (Colorado Springs: Multnomah, 2011), 10.

11. Piper, *Desiring God*, 10.

Chapter 10

1. Dallas Willard, *Spirit of the Disciplines* (San Francisco: Harper-Collins, 1988), 92.

2. Willard, *Spirit of the Disciplines*, 156.

3. Willard, *Spirit of the Disciplines*, 156.

4. Xalavier Nelson Jr., "*Jesus at the Joystick*: Can Video Games be Spiritual?," *Theology of Work Project*, October 10, 2021, https://www.theologyofwork.org/makingitwork/episode/jesus-at-the-joystick-can-video-games-be-spiritual-xalavier-nelson-jr.

5. Nelson, "*Jesus at the Joystick*."

Chapter Appendix 1

1. John Piper, "What Is Worship?," *Desiring God*, April 29, 2016, https://www.desiringgod.org/interviews/what-is-worship.

2. Storms, "Praise."

3. Matthew Kaemingk and Cory B. Willson, *Work and Worship: Reconnecting Our Labor and Liturgy* (Grand Rapids: Baker Academic, 2020).

4. Van Sloten, *Every Job a Parable*, 207.

Chapter Appendix 2

1. Van Sloten, *Every Job a Parable*, 48–50.

2. Carey Nieuwhof, "Why We Need More Entrepreneurial Church Leaders, Not More Shepherds," accessed January 25, 2022, https://careynieuwhof.com/why-we-need-more-entrepreneurial-church-leaders-not-more-shepherds/.

Chapter Appendix 3

1. Doug Sherman and William Hendricks, *Your Work Matters to God* (Colorado Springs: NavPress, 1987), 16.

2. Van Sloten, *Every Job a Parable*.

3. Issler, "Exploring the Pervasive References to Work in Jesus' Parables," 323–39.